9/93

FOR
NUMBER
CRUNCHERS
& Other
Quantitative Types

D0037268

FOR
NUMBER
CRUNCHERS
& Other
Quantitative Types

Rebecca Burnett

VGM Career Horizons
a division of *NTC Publishing Group*
Lincolnwood, Illinois USA

Library of Congress Cataloging-in-Publication Data

Burnett, Rebecca E.,
    Careers for number crunchers & other quantitative types / Rebecca
E. Burnett.

        p.   cm. — (VGM careers for you series)
    Includes bibliographical references.
    ISBN 0–8442–8136–0 — ISBN 0–8442–8137–9 (soft)
    1. Mathematics—Vocational guidance. 2. Statistics—Vocational
guidance. 3. Business mathematics—Vocational guidance. I. Title.
II. Title: Careers for number crunchers and other quantitative
types. III. Series.
QA10.5.B87   1992
510'.23—dc20   92–24334
                                                             CIP

Published by VGM Career Horizons, a division of NTC Publishing Group.
© 1993 by NTC Publishing Group, 4255 West Touhy Avenue,
Lincolnwood (Chicago), Illinois 60646-1975 U.S.A.
Manufactured in the United States of America.

2 3 4 5 6 7 8 9 0 VP 9 8 7 6 5 4 3 2 1

Dedication

To my son, Bob, a number cruncher
in spirit and profession.

Contents

About the Author

Rebecca E. Burnett is an assistant professor of Rhetoric and Professional Communication at Iowa State University where she teaches graduate and undergraduate courses in technical communication and rhetorical analysis. She also has many years of experience as a high school teacher and as a writer. Her primary research involves examining individual and social factors that affect coauthors' collaborative planning of documents. Recently she also has explored writers' uses of metaphor in technical and scientific texts.

She frequently consults in industry and conducts seminars for business. She also serves as a consultant for national education projects; most recently these projects have included computers in the writing curriculum and a video-supported applied communication program for vocational-technical students.

She is either author or coauthor of four texts in literature, composition, and technical communication, including her second edition of *Technical Communication*. Burnett has an M.A. and a Ph.D. from Carnegie-Mellon University, an M.Ed. from the University of Massachusetts—Lowell, and a B.A. from the University of Massachusetts—Amherst.

When she's not doing research, teaching, consulting, or writing, she tries to find time to photograph interesting people and places, attend plays and concerts, fish and sail, cross-country ski, read books with no socially redeeming value, cook, and linger over wonderful meals with friends enjoying leisurely conversations.

Acknowledgments

Brian Beckman	Senior Actuarial Analyst, Country Mutual Insurance
Shelva Boyd	Teacher, Fellows Elementary School
Merle Brendeland	Purchasing Manager, Sauer-Sundstrand Company
Hollace L. Bristol	Associate Professor of Mathematics, Northwestern Connecticut Community College
Chris Burnett	Independent Consulting Forester
Margaret Burnett	Garden Designer for Country Estates
Robert Carosso	Staff Engineer, Bull Worldwide Information Systems
Janet Clemmensen	Senior Systems Analyst, Iowa Lottery
Albert Cuoco	Albert Cuoco, Jr., CPA
Pam Daale	Meteorologist, WOI-TV
Deborah L. Duke	Independent Computer Consultant
Robin Dye	Senior Sales Manager, Newark Electronics
Lisa Ettlinger	Senior Major Account Representative, MCI
Mike Farley	City Administrator, Huxley, Iowa

Lee Foster	Sales Representative, Contractor and Retail Lumber Sales, Chagnon Lumber and Home Center
James Gill	Vice-President of Finance, SECDonohue, Inc.
Arnel Hallauer	Plant Breeder and Geneticist, ISU
Connie Hilts	Office Manager/Bookkeeper, Jim Wagner, Inc., Lincoln-Mercury-Nissan
Dean Isaacson	Head, Department of Statistics, ISU
Elgin Johnston	Professor of Mathematics, ISU
Edward S. Kapron	Financial Advisor, Prudential Securities
Dale Keever	Marketing Research Manager, Iowa Lottery
Steve King	Chief Financial Officer, Iowa Lottery
Carol Leininger	Clinical Research Statistician, Sandoz Pharma AG
Sarah J. Madison	Senior Account Executive, Waddell & Reed
Charles Maurer	District Counsel, Internal Revenue Service
Shelli Munn	Office Manager, Munn's Building Center
Mike Ness	Director of Materials Management, Mary Greeley Medical Center
Marit Nilsen-Hamilton	Professor of Biochemistry, ISU
Kay North	Coordinator K-12/Resource Teacher of Gifted Students, Ames Community Schools
Sarah Nusser	Professor in Charge, Survey Section, Statistical Lab; Assistant Professor, ISU Department of Statistics
Lauri Platter	Buyer Trainee, Fareway Stores, Inc.

Dale Rahfeldt	Registered Investment Advisor and Certified Financial Planner, Rahfeldt Counseling and Instructional Service
Kelli Sampson	Mortgage Loan Sales Representative, Midland Savings Bank
Sam Shaver	Decorative Housewares Buyer, Younkers Department Stores
David Slaughter	President and Chief Executive Officer, ISU Credit Union
Don Stanford	Director of International Marketing, MIT Press
Brent C. Stearns	Sales Agent and Agency Manager, Shelter Insurance
Gary Tarcy	Scientific Associate, Alcoa Technical Center, Aluminum Company of America
Jennifer Taub-Conville	Tax Manager, Continental Cablevision, Inc.
Becky Tschantz	Customer Service Representative, Ames Savings Bank
Tony Vander Zyl	Math Teacher, Ames High School
Mary Beth Willis	Assistant Manager, Midland Savings Bank

Foreword

Number crunchers are a unique breed. They appreciate the subtleties of statistics; they enjoy the logic of complex mathematical formulas. For number crunchers, quantitative puzzles are a challenge, not a chore.

If you share this enthusiasm for numbers, you may be looking for ways to apply your mathematical skills to a new career. If so, your options are nearly limitless. Finance, education, forestry, scientific research: every field needs number crunchers. Number crunchers balance our books; they predict the weather; they observe new scientific phenomena. So whatever your ultimate job description, developing and applying your number-crunching know-how can lead you to an exciting new career.

The Editors of VGM

CHAPTER ONE

Careers for Number Crunchers: Where the Jobs Are

ould you just as soon work with numbers instead of words? While your friends struggle with calculators, do you solve problems in your head? Do you like to manipulate numbers—balancing equations, solving puzzles, calculating odds and probabilities? Do people seek you out because you're good with numbers, asking you to teach them how to approach a problem or interpret the tax tables?

This book will help you decide if a career with numbers is what you want. You have a great many choices about the forum you choose to work in—private business and industry; the public sector (local, state, or federal government); and nonprofit organizations. You also have a range of choices in the fields; a few fields include accounting, banking, engineering, insurance, marketing, medicine, securities, and investments. And finally, you have choices about combining the forum and the field. For example, you can work as a statistician for the U.S. Department of Labor or for Prudential Securities. You can work as an accountant for the Internal Revenue Service or for General Electric. You can teach computer science in a local high school or for the

1

U.S. Navy. You can work as an appraiser for your local real estate tax board or for your state's Division of Natural Resources. You can work as the budget director for Pew Charitable Trusts or for the local community college. In other words, your possibilities are wide open. This book talks about number-crunching careers by looking at some of the fields you can study and work in because most of these fields have jobs in public, private, and nonprofit forums.

Overall Requirements

In general, people who choose the jobs described in *Careers for Number Crunchers & Other Quantitative Types* need a facility with numbers. However, they also need some other important skills: the ability to think logically; the habit of neat, orderly work; and effective skills in oral and written communication. Over and over again, the professionals interviewed for this book stressed that understanding and communicating quantitative concepts were more important than being able to manipulate the numbers. They saw number crunching as a means to an end, necessary but not the end in itself.

Jobs Tracking Debits and Credits

If you're interested in accounting, you might be well suited for a job that involves tracking debits and credits. The jobs introduced in chapter 2 range from being a bookkeeper for an auto dealer to being an accountant who owns his own company, from a tax manager for a national corporation to an attorney for the IRS. The most recent figures from the U.S. Department of Labor's Bureau of Labor Statistics indicate that positions in accounting are likely to increase during the 1990s.

Jobs Managing Money and Cash Flow

A large number of careers require that you be skillful at managing money and cash flow. In general, such jobs involve not only keeping track of how money is spent but also making recommendations about how to spend it. The jobs introduced in chapter 3 range from a city administrator in a small Midwest community to a chief financial officer for a state lottery, from an office manager for a building supplies business to a bank teller.

Jobs Guiding Investments

If you're interested in the stock market and like the idea of investigating the potential growth of a company, you might enjoy a career that involves guiding investments. You might want to be a Wall Street account executive working for a major brokerage house. However, the same skills are necessary for the person who works as an independent financial advisor. Chapter 4 includes discussion of jobs such as mortgage officer, account executive, financial advisor, and credit counselor. The number of positions in fields such as securities and financial sales will moderately increase in the 1990s as a result of the growing array and complexity of financial products.

Jobs Buying in the Workplace

If you like the pressure and excitement of working with people in a fast-paced environment as much as you like working with numbers, you might consider a career in which you will be buying. Chapter 5 identifies jobs such as buyers and purchasing agents. According to the most recent figures from the U.S. Department of Labor's Bureau of Labor Statistics, the 1990s will see a moderate decrease in some buying jobs due to mergers and acquisitions and the trend toward direct shipment to retailers.

The exception is buyers for grocery stores, since mergers and direct shipment do not affect this industry as drastically as they do others.

Jobs Marketing and Selling in the Workplace

People involved in some aspect of marketing or selling usually are confident and outgoing and able to get along with people. Chapter 6 identifies jobs in marketing research, retail and commercial sales, and insurance. According to the most recent figures from the U.S. Department of Labor's Bureau of Labor Statistics, the 1990s will see a moderate increase in the number of some kinds of sales jobs such as real estate agents, brokers, and managers due to growth in professional management of commercial and residential properties, condominiums, and community associations.

Jobs Applying Quantitative Thinking

Many careers focus on problems that require numeric calculations and manipulations as part of the solutions. If this sort of mathematic investigation appeals to you, then you might enjoy using quantitative design as part of your work. In chapter 7 you'll learn about the quantitative aspects of various kinds of computer programming and engineering. The need for many types of engineers and technicians will increase throughout the 1990s. For example, more electrical and electronics engineers as well as electrical and electronics technicians will be needed because of the increasing pace of innovation and the growing importance of electronics in many industries.

Jobs Calculating Probabilities and Risks

Maybe you've always wondered how insurance companies set rates depending on the demographic characteristics of their customers. If problems such as these interest you, then maybe a career calculating probability and risk would give you the opportunity to solve similar problems. Chapter 8 describes jobs you might consider as an actuary or a statistician. One reason more statisticians will be needed in the 1990s is because of the increasing application of statistical techniques to improve quality control. More actuaries will be needed in part because insurance policies are increasing in number and complexity.

Jobs Investigating the Biological and Physical Universe

Careers that focus on investigating the physical universe enable you to pursue interests in physical and biological natural sciences, all of which require some quantitative skills. Chapter 9 introduces a range of careers including work as a biochemist, forester, plant geneticist, and meteorologist. Figures from the Bureau of Labor Statistics indicate that the number of professionals needed in all of these fields is going to increase during the 1990s.

Jobs Sharing Number-Crunching Know-How

Some people gain a tremendous amount of satisfaction by sharing number-crunching know-how. Chapter 10 deals primarily with jobs for teaching math and computer science in elementary schools, secondary schools, community colleges, and universities. The 1990s will see some increase in the need for additional teachers.

Jobs Managing Quantitative Careers

Every organization has managers, and these managers have to deal with a number of quantitative elements such as budgets and operations. Chapter 11 concentrates on managers, from a chief executive officer of a credit union to an assistant bank manager, from a vice-president of an environmental consulting company to a director of purchasing for a major medical center. Regardless of the size of an organization, the people at the top are ultimately responsible for everything that happens in their office, division, or department.

Jobs with Number Crunching for Non-Number Crunchers

Not all careers that require quantitative know-how are as obvious as those in accounting or engineering or astronomy. You may prefer a career that requires quantitative skill but sees that skill as distinctly secondary. Chapter 12 focuses on jobs with number crunching for non-number crunchers, which include careers in book publishing, educational administration, and landscape design. All of these fields have positive prospects for growth in the 1990s.

Job Qualifications

Work requiring quantitative skills ranges from entry-level jobs that provide on-the-job training (for example, workers on a manufacturing line who are responsible for checking computer printouts for each production run) to advanced positions that require a Ph.D. (for example, a specialist in bio-mechanical engineering analyzing data about a prosthesis). A few jobs that require quantitative skills are available to high school graduates with no previous experience, though the companies typically provide on-the-job training. Unfortunately, jobs of this type often offer little opportunity for advancement without further training and education. For most careers that require quantitative skills, you need education beyond high school. Vocational-technical schools as well as two-year and four-year colleges offer a variety of programs that provide introductory and advanced coursework. Many programs include co-op jobs and internships so that students get opportunities to put their classroom knowledge into practice. Some jobs also require graduate coursework; master's and doctoral programs offer opportunities for more theoretical study and chances to conduct research.

You don't necessarily have to go from high school to college to graduate school to a job. You can learn quantitative skills in other places. Some people choose to serve in the military where they elect specialized training that may include quantitative skills. Another possibility is to start work for a company that offers excellent in-house training; taking company courses doesn't make up for more formal college courses, but in-house training often provides specialized information that relates immediately to your work.

Having quantitative ability means more than being able to balance your checkbook and do your own income taxes. Quantitative ability is not simply a collection of mechanical skills—being able to rattle off formulas in geometry, calculus, and chemistry, or knowing the multiplication tables through the 20s. Rather it's a way of thinking that includes these mechanical skills but a great deal more as well. This "more" includes understanding *numeracy*. As mathematician John Allen Paulos, author of *Beyond Numeracy*, comments in the introduction to this recent book, "Mathematics . . . provides a way of viewing the world, and developing a mathematical consciousness or outlook can enhance our daily rounds" (p. 3).

Finding a Job

You can locate jobs in a variety of places. Newspaper ads generally are aimed at a broad audience. The advantage of newspaper ads is that they're readily available; however, these ads can't provide much information, and each one may generate hundreds of responses so that your letter and resume may not get a great deal of attention. Ads also appear in many professional journals and newsletters. Although these ads, often for advanced or specialized jobs, go to a narrower audience, they usually have more information about the job. You also can learn about available jobs from agencies—your state's division of employment as well as a range of private professional employment agencies. Unlike state agencies, these private agencies always charge a fee—sometimes to the prospective employee, sometimes to the employer who is looking for a new employee—but they also can be very helpful. You can make direct contact with companies by going to job fairs where companies set up table displays and exhibits so that prospective employees can learn about the company, talk with recruiters, leave copies of a resume, and, in some cases, arrange for an interview. You also can learn about employment possibilities if you subscribe or have access to an electronic bulletin board that lists available jobs with specific companies. One of the most accessible places to learn about jobs is your high school or college placement office. Most placement offices keep up-to-date files about available jobs, often arrange on-campus interviews with recruiters, and keep data sheets and resumes about your experience and education on file for prospective employers to review. Finally, you often learn about the best jobs by word of mouth, through informal networks where someone you know knows someone else who's looking for a person with just your qualifications. So it pays to let people know that you're looking for work.

Future Projections

The U.S. Department of Labor's Bureau of Labor Statistics reports that the 1990s will see a significant increase in the following jobs that involve quantitative skills:

- actuaries
- computer programmers
- computer systems analysts
- data processing equipment repairers
- electrical and electronics engineers
- electrical and electronics technicians and technologists
- management analysts and consultants
- medical record technicians
- meteorologists
- millwrights
- operations research analysts
- programmers—numerical, tool, and process control

The Bureau of Labor Statistics also projects that a number of other jobs that involve quantitative skills will see a moderate increase during the 1990s:

- agricultural and food scientists
- chemical engineers
- electroencephalographic technologists (and others involved in neurodiagnostic testing)
- electromedical and biomedical equipment repairers
- engineering, mathematics, and natural science managers
- geologists, geophysicists, and oceanographers
- industrial engineers (except safety engineers)
- industrial machinery mechanics
- industrial production managers
- mechanical engineers
- metallurgists and metallurgical, ceramic, and materials engineers
- opticians
- petroleum engineers
- pharmacy assistants
- property and real estate managers
- radiologic technologists and technicians
- securities and financial service sales workers
- underwriters

Using This Book

You'll find two kinds of information in this book: facts and case studies. They work together to give you a good sense of what lots of jobs are like.

You'll find *job descriptions,* information about *training and education,* and the *earning potential* for many jobs that have a strong quantitative component. Some of this factual information comes from publications available from specific professional organizations and associations. However, most of it comes from the Bureau of Labor Statistics, which is part of the U.S. Department of Labor. Two of their books are particularly useful: *Occupational Outlook Handbook* and *Outlook 2000.*

The most interesting and useful information, though, comes from the more than forty "In the Workplace . . ." segments that appear throughout the book. These descriptions of real people and their jobs give you a feel for what it might be like to be an accountant, a retail buyer, clinical statistician, or a television meteorologist. Read these case studies carefully; then reread those that interest you the most. The details and examples in them will give you more insight into number-crunching careers than all of the facts in the rest of the book. These stories of real people show you the complexities of the workplace and the hard work that people put into their careers, but they also show people who love what they do and who are constantly challenged and excited by their careers.

Whatever the area of specialization, the more than forty women and men interviewed for this book agree that if you want a career with a strong quantitative emphasis, you should consider the following suggestions:

- take as many science and math courses as you can;
- take courses in business and computer science;
- develop your communication skills in writing, public speaking, and group discussion;
- learn to work effectively as a collaborator and in small groups;

- participate in internships, work-study programs, and apprenticeship programs to gain workplace experience; and
- learn more than the "what." Learn the "why" and the "how."

They all agree that good number crunchers know the reasons for what they're doing, can explain their processes, and can recognize ways to apply their number crunching.

Further Reading

Paulos, John Allen. *Beyond Numeracy: Ruminations of a Numbers Man.* New York: Alfred A. Knopf, 1991.

Tracking Debits and Credits

We know that societies have valued accurate financial record keeping for more than 5,000 years, dating all the way back to ancient Babylonia, Phoenicia, Egypt, and Greece. In fact, some of the earliest written records that exist are agricultural and shipping records. The jobs introduced in this chapter range from accountants and tax attorneys to a variety of financial records processors. Increased productivity in these fields results from widespread use of improved computer technology and software. As computers take over some of the machine operation, the need for entry-level clerks and record keepers will decrease during the 1990s; however, the need for well-educated and trained professionals who understand the processes will increase.

Accountants

Accountants are responsible for preparing or supervising the preparation of all of the financial reports of an organization—for example, profit and loss statements, balance sheets, tax reports. Because accounting is a highly specialized field, you can work in a number of different areas:

- *General accountants* are responsible for the overall financial record keeping of a company.
- *Budget accountants* help to create new budgets within a company and review expenditures to make sure that the budget is followed.
- *Cost accountants* determine the per unit cost of products or services, keeping track of costs for product development, manufacturing, promotion, and distribution, and then considering factors such as equipment depreciation, inflation, and employee benefits.
- *Property accountants* keep records of equipment and property, tracking factors such as depreciation.
- *Systems accountants* design and implement accounting systems for organizations that have special problems.
- *Tax accountants* prepare local, state, and federal tax returns.

Accountants may work in public, private, or government accounting. *Public accountants* work independently or for an accounting firm; they're hired by individuals or companies that want a range of accounting services: preparing tax returns, auditing books, and offering advice about taxes and investments. *Private accountants* (sometimes called management, internal, or industrial accountants) manage the financial records for a specific company that employs them. *Government accountants* work within individual government agencies or departments.

Initial Training

Most accountants and auditors need to have at least a bachelor's degree in accounting or a closely related field. Many employers expect a master's degree in accounting or a master's in business administration with a concentration in accounting.

To be eligible to take a CPA (certified public accountant) exam, candidates must have completed a minimum of 150 hours of college (the equivalent of a five-year bachelor's program or a master's program) and, in most states, must have at least one year of workplace experience. The four-part, 2 1/2-day Uniform CPA Exam is prepared by the American Institute of Certified Public Accountants.

Earning Potential

The most recent edition of the College Placement Council Salary Survey reports that entry-level employees with bachelor's degrees in accounting receive average starting salary offers of $25,300 a year; master's degree entry-level employees, $28,800. These figures are higher than those reported in the most recent issue of the *Occupational Outlook Handbook,* which reported that salaries for beginning public and management accountants and trainee internal auditor accountants were in the $22,000 to $23,500 range. The highest salaries for chief management accountants ranged from $38,000 to nearly $100,000.

In the Workplace as an Accountant

Al Cuoco is the sole proprietor of his own accounting firm, Albert Cuoco, Jr., CPA. His business offers accounting, tax, and related business services to the general public including individuals, partnerships, corporations, and trusts.

BACKGROUND. Al brought a good deal of experience to his own company when he decided to open it six years ago. Al has a bachelor's degree in mathematics and a master's degree in taxation. In addition to being a CPA (certified public accountant), Al is one of about twenty-five CPAs in the country who has passed the exams that enable him to be licensed to practice law in the U.S. Tax Court.

Al's professional career started with the Internal Revenue Service (IRS) where he worked as an agent (later getting promotions to higher grades). He says this job was professional and varied, but very regimented. Although there was a high level of job security, there were also economic restrictions. For example, teaching accounting at a local four-year college—which he has done for many years—was the only allowable form of additional employment. He could not act as a tax consultant or prepare tax returns because of a conflict of interest.

After nine years with the IRS, Al accepted a position as director of taxes for Computervision, Inc., one of the rapid-growth companies in the high-tech loop surrounding Boston in the 1980s. Al says this job was completely different from working for the IRS. High-tech companies are often seen as high-stress environments; Al says the stress is caused, in part, by a company that is growing very rapidly. The job was challenging because of the rapid growth. However, the economic downturn in the Northeast region of the country in the late 1980s resulted in huge layoffs, and the turmoil from those layoffs resulted in corporate reorganization.

Six years ago, Al opened his own business. One of the things he likes most about being his own boss is that he's responsible for his own policies and successes. As sole proprietor, he selects his own clients and makes as much or as little as the time and effort he's willing to expend.

RESPONSIBILITIES.   During a typical year, he prepares tax returns for about 250 individuals, 25 corporations, and 20 various part-nerships and trusts. Al explains that his goal is to "insure that my clients fulfill all of their various tax obligations and maintain adequate records to present financial information to banks, cred-itors, owners, and taxing authorities." These obligations typi-cally include responsibilities for income tax, sales tax, and employment tax.

In order to assist his clients in the accurate and timely com-pletion of their tax returns, Al often helps them identify and organize their financial records. Then he can present this infor-mation in a format that's acceptable for banks or creditors who may use the information to make business judgments or plan strategies. A typical client for Al is a small business that does about $500,000 to $1,000,000 of business a year and has between five and ten employees. The business is usually a sole proprietorship or a partnership that has bank loans and some outside investments, primarily in real estate.

CHALLENGES. The most exciting part of his work comes, Al says, when people buy or sell businesses. These transactions—which include mergers, acquisitions, and reorganizations—tend to be the most complicated. They also tend to involve the most amount of money, which gives him a greater opportunity to save money for his client

Another challenge comes in keeping complicated conflicts with the IRS out of U.S. Tax Court. In practice, he says that "98 percent of the cases never get to trial." Responsible accountants and attorneys often work to reduce the amount of litigation by settling out of court. Usually the IRS is only interested in going to court when the case involves very large sums of money or when it involves a "prime issue"—that is, a precedent-setting case.

SUGGESTIONS. If you want to be an accountant, Al suggests that you take the most rigorous program you can find. He also urges students to take courses in logic and problem solving, which are often offered by departments of philosophy or psychology. "When you graduate, first work for the IRS or for a very large public accounting firm because of the great breadth of experience that you gain. Not only is this experience looked on favorably when you move to another position, but you'll have an opportunity to meet potential clients you might work for later."

Attorneys

Many attorneys deal with quantitative matters in their roles as advisors and advocates. For example, attorneys may specialize in insurance, contract negotiations, trusts, mortgages, or taxes. Other specializations also may involve quantitative elements; for example, a communications lawyer representing public utilities may appear before the Federal Energy Regulatory Commission to testify about utility rates.

Initial Training

All attorneys must be licensed, which nearly always involves passing a bar exam and an ethics exam. To be eligible to take the bar exam, a person must complete at least three years of college and graduate from law school, which takes another three years. The Multistate Bar Exam is required in forty-six states (all except Indiana, Iowa, Louisiana, and Washington) in addition to what is typically a six-hour locally prepared state bar exam, which may include a three-hour essay exam (the MSEE—Multistate Essay Exam).

Students interested in a particular aspect of the law will probably find related courses useful. For example, engineering and science courses could be useful for a prospective patent attorney; accounting could be useful for a future tax attorney. As you'll see below, some tax attorneys also earn a degree in accounting.

Earning Potential

The most recent edition of the *Occupational Outlook Handbook* reports that salaries for beginning attorneys in private industry average about $34,000. However, graduates from top law schools may start with salaries over $80,000 a year. Beginning attorneys working for the federal government started at approximately $29,000. A number of factors affect this broad range of salaries: academic record; specialization; and type, size, and location of the employer.

In the Workplace as a Tax Attorney

Jennifer Taub-Conville works as tax manager in Continental Cablevision's corporate headquarters in Boston. Continental Cablevision, Inc., which provides cable television to almost three million U.S. subscribers, has $1 billion in annual sales.

BACKGROUND.   Jennifer set out to be an environmental lawyer, having earned a B.S. in environmental science before she went to law school. However, once she was actually in law school, she became more interested in tax law and decided to concentrate in taxation, taking courses such as corporate taxation, and liquidation and mergers. Why tax law? Jennifer says she has "always had strong mathematics skills for number crunching. Law school provided me with the ability to use those skills to analyze tax problems and do research."

After graduating from law school, Jennifer worked as a tax analyst for Arthur Anderson & Company where she was primarily responsible for preparing and reviewing clients' tax returns and for conducting tax research. While she worked as a tax analyst, she also completed an M.A. in accounting, concentrating in personal and corporate taxation. After three years, Jennifer accepted a position as tax manager with Continental Cablevision, partly because she liked their corporate philosophy of teamwork and sharing, and partly because she wanted the opportunity for a job with increased responsibility and a high degree of independence.

RESPONSIBILITIES. At Continental Cablevision, Jennifer has a number of responsibilities. She says that approximately 40 percent of her work involves tax planning, tax forecasting, and tax research. Her forecasting allows the future tax position of the company to be estimated, which contributes to well-timed business decisions. For example, tax forecasting can help determine the most beneficial periods in which an investment should be sold or a new system acquired. Jennifer also conducts research in various tax areas—partnerships, corporate tax, property tax, and sales tax—that affect the day-to-day operations of Continental Cablevision.

Another 25 percent of Jennifer's time is spent working on the tax analysis of mergers, acquisitions, and investments. She reviews the possible tax ramifications of proposed mergers and acquisitions and works with corporate attorneys to ensure proper tax disclosures and indemnifications. Another 25 percent of her time is spent supervising and reviewing the preparation of corporate tax returns by the four professionals in Continental

Cablevision's tax department. The final 10 percent of Jennifer's job involves working with cable associations such as the National Cable Television Association in Washington, DC, on tax legislation as it affects the cable industry. For example, she worked with colleagues in other cable television companies to coordinate the cable industry's position on proposed changes in the tax laws. Then she met with representatives from the administrative arm of the U.S. Treasury to present the cable industry's position on the proposed changes.

CHALLENGES. In explaining her work, Jennifer says, "Numbers are behind what I do, but the majority of my job involves research analysis, memo writing, and theorizing—working on a conceptual level." She applies this research to practical situations. For example, recently Jennifer had meetings over a three-month period with the tax counsel for an investment group who wanted to invest $400 million in Continental Cablevision. The tax counsel for the group wanted to be able to assume a level of comfort about Continental Cablevision's tax liabilities. Acting as Continental Cablevision's representative during their various conversations and meetings, Jennifer advised the investment group's tax counsel about the cable industry's position on IRS policies and substantiated Continental Cablevision's historic and current tax positions.

SUGGESTIONS. Jennifer says that she loves her job, but that it's hard work, the hours are demanding, and keeping informed of tax law changes is an ongoing part of a tax professional's life. Jennifer regularly takes continuing education courses offered by law and accounting associations in specialized areas of tax law such as mergers and acquisitions and international tax. Anyone interested in tax law needs a strong ability to analyze, to negotiate, to understand the interplay of numbers in applied situations. Too many people overestimate the importance of mathematical calculations to conduct analyses and underestimate the importance of being able both to write reports that clearly describe and explain these analyses, and review and draw implications from research.

In the Workplace as an IRS Attorney

The overall function of the office of Chief Counsel of the Internal Revenue Service (IRS) is separated into three areas: collection, prosecution, and litigation. Charles Maurer is an attorney with nearly twenty years experience in the office of the IRS District Counsel. His primary responsibility is to provide legal advice to the IRS and represent the commissioner of the IRS in tax court. He describes his job as having three primary functions: First, attorneys in his office are involved in the collection of tax liabilities. Second, they are involved in the criminal prosecution of individuals and corporations who violate criminal statutes. Third, they are involved in civil cases with the IRS Examination Division, which attempts to determine if people or companies owe more than they have reported.

Charles differentiates the work of the district counsel, which involves lawyers handling litigation, from the work of the district director, which involves accountants handling audits. Audits are part of an administrative process; people or companies with tax returns that may have potential problems receive a Statutory Notice of Deficiency. The office of the District Counsel may review the notice before it is issued. The individual or company receiving the notice may then go to tax court, where Charles or one of his colleagues represents the IRS.

BACKGROUND.   Charles started work for the IRS after earning a bachelor's degree in history and a J. D. when he graduated from law school. Like other attorneys new to the IRS, he took part in the IRS initial training program; he went to one-to-two week training sessions during his first year. Since then he has regularly participated in annual three-to-four day regional training programs for updates about new issues and programs related to legal aspects of taxation. He also takes part in ongoing training for specialized cases and interests. Continuing legal education is available through colleges as well as from professional organizations such as the bar association. Charles is involved in insurance cases, so he makes it a special point to attend two or three insurance industry training sessions every year.

RESPONSIBILITIES. The largest amount of Charles's time—he estimates up to 40 percent—is taken up by trial preparation, working on the details of specific litigation. The actual litigation takes only about 5 percent of his time. The remainder of Charles's time is spent as an advisor for the IRS District Director's office where he my work on one big case or many small cases. Less experienced IRS attorneys usually work on simple cases and are also members of a team with highly experienced attorneys, such as Charles, to examine corporations. Having an accounting background is an advantage for IRS attorneys, but the lack of it is not a disadvantage. Charles says that in his work the quantities and the relationships—that is, the proportions—are often far more important than specific mathematical calculations. An IRS attorney deals with lots of conceptual quantitative work, which involves identifying numeric trends and patterns.

Financial Record Processors

Financial record processors include a range of jobs: billing clerks, bookkeepers, accounting and auditing clerks, and payroll and timekeeping clerks.

Initial Training

Financial record processors are high school graduates who have vocational training in accounting, bookkeeping, or business data processing. They also may have training from postsecondary vocational schools, community and junior colleges, and business schools. A few companies will hire individuals who have no formal training in financial record processing and depend on on-the-job training to teach them the necessary skills.

Earning Potential

The most recent issue of the *Occupational Outlook Handbook* reports that the median income for financial record processors is $16,000. The lowest 10 percent earn less than $10,500, the middle 50 percent earn between $13,000 and $20,500, and the top 10 percent earn more than $25,500.

In the Workplace as an Office Manager/Bookkeeper

Connie Hilts works as an office manager for Jim Wagner, Inc., a Lincoln-Mercury-Nissan auto dealer that typically sells between eighty-five and ninety cars each month. She's completely responsible for all of the company's bookkeeping: accounts payable, payroll, accounts receivable, and the quarterly and annual financial statements.

This year her job became much more streamlined when the company installed a new integrated computer system. Although it took everyone at Jim Wagner, Inc., about a month of training and adjustment, Connie says they now function smoothly with a system that has sharply reduced the amount of paperwork in every department. She says there are virtually no handwritten records of shop time in the service department, daily balances of cash, or inventory for parts for new and used cars; it's all done on the computer.

BACKGROUND. Connie started working as a bookkeeper right out of high school. In high school, she took lots of math (algebra, trigonometry, geometry, and calculus) and accounting courses. While she was still in high school, she also took a course in advanced accounting at a local college. Her first job was as a bookkeeper for an insurance company, where she handled the agents' accounts. After two years, she accepted a position as a bookkeeper for a jewelry store. Then, two years later, she started working as the bookkeeper for Jim Wagner, Inc., where she's been for the past ten years.

RESPONSIBILITIES.   The new computer system has cut her work-load and shifted her role so that now she functions "more as an auditor" than a bookkeeper. She estimates, in fact, that about one-third of her time is spent auditing what everyone else does. She reviews the work of employees in the service department, in the parts department, in new and used car sales, and for the title clerk. For example, she confirms that expenses are charged to the correct accounts. Another third of her time is spent managing accounts payable. Invoices are posted daily and paid monthly. The remaining third of her time is spent doing a variety of tasks: weekly and biweekly payroll, costing new and used car deals, calculating commissions, preparing quarterly reports.

Connie emphasizes that "doing books is a lot more involved than what you learn in class. Quirky situations come up that the bookkeeper has to handle." She explains, as an example, that the Lincoln-Mercury franchise does things very differently from the Nissan franchise, so she really has to keep two sets of records that then need to be combined for quarterly reports. She says that a bookkeeper gets things "after the fact" and is expected to "make things right."

SUGGESTIONS.   Anyone considering a career as a bookkeeper or office manager needs to have computer experience. Connie says it's the "A#1 most important thing." You need to know basic computer applications and functions as well as understand how computer systems work. Connie says it's also important to pay attention to details. "Having an account balance within three or four cents isn't enough. Debits and credits always balance." Finally, Connie says that it's not enough to be good with num-bers; you have to have an overall sense how business works— business in general and the business you work for in particular. "There are so many gray lines about what is an asset or an expense; it takes knowledge and experience to know what's allowable. . . . It's not so cut and dried as the textbooks say."

Addresses for Further Information

Career information about certified public accounting and CPA standards and examinations:

American Institute of Certified Public Accountants
    1211 Avenue of the Americas
    New York, NY 10036-8775

Career information about specialized fields of accounting and auditing:

National Association of Accountants
    10 Paragon Drive
    Montvale, NJ 07645

National Society of Public Accountants and the Accreditation
    Council for Accountancy
    1010 North Fairfax Street
    Alexandria, VA 22314

The Institute of Internal Auditors
    249 Maitland Avenue
    Altamonte Springs, FL 32701-4201

The EDP Auditors Association
    P. 0. Box 88180
    Carol Stream, IL 60188-0180

Career information about accredited accounting programs and educational institutions offering a specialization in accounting or business management:

American Assembly of Collegiate Schools of Business
    605 Old Ballas Road
    Suite 220
    St. Louis, MO 63141

Legal information and information about applying to law school:

Association of American Law Schools
  1 Dupont Circle NW
  Suite 370 '
  Washington, DC 20036

Brochure describing careers as bookkeepers or accounting clerks:

Association of Independent Colleges and Schools
  1 Dupont Circle NW
  Suite 350
  Washington, DC 20036

CHAPTER THREE

Managing Money and Cash Flow

M oney managers in an organization—whether it be a public agency, a private retail business, a city government, or a nonprofit foundation—oversee the flow of cash, establish and supervise financial policies and procedures, and assess the organization's financial status. While the money managers such as chief financial officers are at the top of an organization, many other people handle the cash flow within an organization and ensure that budgets are followed and money is correctly dispersed. For example, office managers are often responsible for day-to-day financial operations and the preparation of financial reports. Similarly, bank tellers not only handle a great deal of money every day, but they need to know the bank's policies and procedures for many different types of transactions.

Managing Money at the Top

The specific job titles, of course, vary from organization to organization, but generally financial managers fall into these broad categories. *Treasurers* or *chief financial officers* oversee the financial management of all departments or divisions in an organization, working with managers to develop policies and supervise the implementation of those policies. *Controllers* (called *comptrollers* in some companies) direct the preparation of all financial documents such as income statements and balance sheets. They also oversee the preparation of financial reports by budget analysts, auditors, and accountants.

Other kinds of money managers are also important to the financial well-being of an organization.

- *Cash managers* monitor the cash receipts and disbursements, manage loans, and track a variety of other financial instruments.
- *Risk and insurance managers* work to make sure that organizations don't suffer undue risks or losses as a result of financial transactions, investments, or operations.
- *Credit managers* (including credit card managers) establish credit rating criteria, determine credit ceilings, and monitor their own organization's policies and practices about extending credit.
- *Reserve officers* supervise an organization's purchase and sale of a variety of securities such as bonds in order to maintain an appropriate asset-liability ratio.

Every kind of financial institution has financial managers— bank managers, savings and loan association managers, credit union managers, and finance company managers—all of whom know all about the finances of their own organization. But they also need to know a great deal about allied industries. For example, a bank manager would need to know about insurance, real estate, and securities as well as about practices in business and industry.

General Managers and Top Executives

General managers and other top executives are the decision makers of an organization. Top executives may be department store managers, superintendents of schools, or chiefs of police. Top executives work together with an organization's chief executive officer and the board of directors to establish the organization's general goals, formulate policies, and direct the implementation of those policies. Although top executives delegate many specific functions, they are ultimately responsible for what happens in their section of an organization.

Initial Training

General managers and other top executives generally have at least a bachelor's degree in liberal arts or business administration. Their major is often related to the departments they manage—for example, a major in computer science for a general manager of data processing. Many top executives have graduate and professional degrees. Typically, managers in administrative, marketing, financial, or manufacturing activities have an M.B.A. Managers in highly technical manufacturing areas and in research often have a master's or doctoral degree in an engineering or scientific specialty. Similarly, a law degree would be expected for general managers of corporate legal departments, and a master's degree in health services administration might be expected for a hospital administrator.

The key to gaining a top executive position, however, is not only academic training; it's experience that builds on this initial training. Although many top executives continue to attend professional seminars and training sessions, they generally have their jobs because of other factors such as expert-level knowledge, leadership skills, motivation, flexibility, self-confidence, and problem-solving and decision-making abilities.

Earning Potential

The most recent edition of the *Occupational Outlook Handbook* reports that the median income for general managers and top executives is approximately $38,700. Many earn considerably more than $52,000, depending on factors such as the level of responsibility and the type, size, and location of the firm. General managers and top executives often receive additional compensation in the form of bonuses, stock awards, and cash-equivalent fringe benefits such as company-paid insurance premiums or the use of a company car.

Chief Financial Officers

The chief financial officer (CFO) of an organization is responsible for maintaining the fiscal health of an organization and, thus, oversees all the financial aspects of that organization. This individual establishes and implements the organization's financial policies, often in conjunction with other officers of the organization.

Initial Training

Chief financial officers (CFOs) are a specialized category of top executive who generally have at least a bachelor's degree in finance or accounting or in business administration with a concentration in finance or accounting. Many CFOs also have a Master of Business Administration (M.B.A.) or a master's degree in finance or accounting. Many also will have passed professional certification exams in accounting, auditing, and information systems.

Earning Potential

The most recent edition of the *Occupational Outlook Handbook* reports that the median income for CFOs and other financial managers is $32,800. The lowest 10 percent earn $17,500 or less; the top 10 percent earn over $52,000. Higher salaries are more likely in large organizations and in cities.

In the Workplace as a Chief Financial Officer

Steve King is the chief financial officer (CFO) for the Iowa Lottery, overseeing all the financial aspects of a state government organization with approximately $150 million in annual sales.

BACKGROUND. Steve came to this position after eight years in the State Auditor's Office, where he was most recently an audit manager of the EDP (Electronic Data Processing) Auditing Section. Steve's B.S. is in management and accounting, and he has passed his CPA (Certified Public Accountant) exams and at one time held auditing certifications: CIA (Certified Internal Auditor) and CISA (Certified Information Systems Auditor). But no amount of academic coursework would be sufficient preparation for this job that includes everything from responsibility for internal financial management to involvement in the user and statistical testing of new lottery games, what they call "systems acceptance testing." When Steve took this new position, he also assumed the responsibility for designing the job and acquiring the on-the-job training necessary to get it done.

RESPONSIBILITIES. Steve talks with enthusiasm about his job as CFO, explaining the enjoyment he gets out of helping design products that are fun. He says he suspects that the pleasure of creating this kind of product seeps over into the day-to-day operation of the job, creating a unique atmosphere. Despite the technical nature of Steve's job, he spends only 35 to 40 percent of his time using his quantitative skills. In fact, he says that because of the correspondence and reports that he has to write, he uses his word processor more than he uses his spreadsheet. Another chunk of his time, 15 to 20 percent, is spent dealing with personnel issues—for example, meeting with the union steward to resolve potential problems. He also is responsible for overseeing the duties of a secretary as well as the Lottery's accounting supervisor and validation supervisor, who are each responsible for a half-dozen employees.

CHALLENGES. Steve likes his job, especially the challenges that come with problem solving. One of his strengths is his ability to solve problems that have no easy answers. He admits that he enjoys looking at problems from different directions, and he says he tries for an equal balance of conceptualization and number crunching. First he conceptualizes a way to handle the problem; then he runs the numbers. For example, before the Lottery introduced a new game with a fixed-dollar amount for the top prize ($100,000), he worked with colleagues to come up with alternative scenarios. What would happen if a great many people over a long period of time happened to hit on the right combination of numbers? Could the Lottery pay out without long-term problems? Steve ran 1,000 two-year scenarios through the computer (the scenarios were based on random number generations of winners) before he decided that having a fixed top prize could work. This kept the players happy and the Lottery solvent. He tempers stubbornness with creativity, considering a range of creative options as he works at a situation until all the issues surrounding it are resolved and, he hopes, all of the ramifications have been considered.

City Managers and City Administrators

City managers are responsible for all municipal operations including hiring and firing. They also are responsible for the police department. In contrast, city administrators have a slightly different job; they are responsible for all municipal operations except hiring and firing and do not have to manage the police department, which is usually the mayor's responsibility.

Initial Training

City managers and administrators generally have at least a bachelor's degree in finance or accounting, or in business administration with a concentration in finance or accounting. Many also have either a Master of Business Administration degree (M.B.A.) or a Master of Public Administration degree (M.P.A.).

Earning Potential

The most recent edition of the *Occupational Outlook Handbook* reports that the median income for city managers and administrators is $32,800. The lowest 10 percent earn $17,500 or less; the top 10 percent earn over $52,000. Higher salaries are more likely in large organizations and in cities.

In the Workplace as a City Administrator

Mike Farley is the city administrator for Huxley, Iowa (population 2,047). As the chief financial officer, he is responsible for developing and administering the budget. He also is responsible for supervising personnel (except for the police department), managing city operations, and administering the policies and procedures.

BACKGROUND.   Mike didn't have a direct path from high school to college to city administration. After high school, he spent a year in the U.S. Navy. After an honorable discharge, he spent another ten years doing a variety of jobs: working as a union carpenter, doing retail work, and managing a muffler shop. But then he decided to use his G.I. bill to go to college. He was fascinated by what he learned about planning and politics in the public sector, so he earned his B.S. in community and regional planning. By this time he had developed a strong interest in city management, so he went on to earn an M.P.A. (Master of Public Administration), with a focus on small town administration.

His first job after college was as city administrator/clerk in Preston, a small town (population 1,200) in eastern Iowa. From there, he worked as one of four department heads in Sheldon (population 5,000), Iowa. As community development director in Sheldon, he was responsible for the community's economic development program, which involved writing grants and attracting new businesses. In his current job as city administrator for Huxley, Mike estimates that as much as 75 percent of his job involves quantitative work. He says, "With most things, a manager needs to know how much money and time something takes.

When I'm talking to a community group, I try to put things in basic quantitative terms in relation to that audience."

RESPONSIBILITIES. Every year Mike starts the budget process for the next fiscal year (July 1–June 30) in October, creating a plan for balancing revenues and expenditures. He sets up the projected budget on a computer, using Lotus software as well as interactive budget and accounting software. Using MBO (management by objective) and ZBB (zero-based budgeting) techniques and providing a three-year history of that department's budget, he encourages department heads and other city employees to get involved with defining their goals and objectives and then identifying expenditures to meet them. He asks department heads to justify the line items in their budgets and to give a rationale for any increases. By mid-January, Mike knows the amounts he can expect from his seven primary sources of revenue. For example, a significant portion of the city's $1.4 million budget comes from the general fund (sources such as property taxes). Other revenue sources include a local option tax (1 percent of the state's 5 percent sales tax) and a road-use tax. Mike meets twice a month with the city council for public hearings; in January and February, these hearings are to iron out any concerns about the budget, so by the end of February, the budget for the upcoming fiscal year is set.

CHALLENGES. Mike says that although he didn't have many undergraduate or graduate math courses, he did take several useful statistics courses and has had lots of on-the-job training. For example, he's learned a great deal from city clerks, bankers, and specialized attorneys such as the city's bond counsel. (A bond counsel knows the financial implications of state statutes and advises municipalities about financing instruments of different kinds.) For a city administrator, expenditures need to be justified, whether for personnel or supplies. Mike gets to apply quantitative and problem-solving skills to different situations every day. Right now he's working on a problem facing many other municipalities—how to manage the approximately 16 percent annual increase in costs related to health care, such as medical insurance and workmen's compensation for city employees.

Handling the Cash Flow in an Organization

While the CFOs and managers design financial systems and oversee the construction of budgets, many small businesses are run by office managers who handle the day-to-day financial decisions and cash flow as well as take responsibility for quarterly and annual financial reports. Although many banking procedures and transactions are now computerized (electronic transfers are common and ATMs—automatic teller machines—are everywhere), bank tellers are still essential, and, in reality, many people prefer dealing with a friendly and knowledgeable professional rather than a machine.

Office Manager

Most office managers are responsible for supervising the office staff, maintaining bookkeeping records, and keeping track of a variety of aspects of the organization's operation, ranging from overseeing employee benefits to filing reports related to worker injury with the insurance company, worker's compensation, and OSHA.

Initial Training

Although many clerical supervisors and office managers have a high school diploma and lots of experience, many employers now prefer an associate's degree or, in some cases, a bachelor's degree. Certainly computer experience is essential for most supervisory or managerial positions. But more important than the coursework is the experience—expertise about the business as well as the ability to give and follow orders. Supervisors and managers not only need to be flexible and have good human relations skills, they also need to be able to set priorities, be highly organized, and pay close attention to detail.

Earning Potential

The median earnings of full-time clerical supervisors and office managers, according to information in the most recent edition of the *Occupational Outlook Handbook,* are approximately $23,700. The middle 50 percent earn between $17,700 and $31,800 a year. The lowest 10 percent earn less than $14,000. The top 10 percent earn over $42,700. Many supervisors and managers also receive a variety of fringe benefits.

In the Workplace as an Office Manager

Shelli Munn is the office manager (as well as a corporate officer) for Munn's Building Center—a lumberyard and building center.

BACKGROUND. The job that Shelli has is often done by someone with a two-year degree in business or bookkeeping. However, Shelli has a B.B.A. (a bachelor's degree in business administration) in accounting. She learned some parts of the job—particularly the day-to-day bookkeeping functions such as preparing payroll and sales tax reports—once she was on the job.

For other aspects of her job, such as putting together financial statements, she was well-prepared. She attributes a great deal of her preparation to taking useful courses. In addition to taking accounting and finance classes, Shelli says several other courses have been extremely valuable, including an introduction to management information systems (MIS), both theoretical and applied auditing, and an English course in business writing. In the management part of her job, she also uses what she learned in a course in quantitative approaches to business; using EOQ (economic order quantity) enables her to identify variables such as item cost, freight cost, lead time, and storage space and then conduct a ratio analysis to help determine the amount of an item that should be ordered each time.

She started working at Munn's as a part-time bookkeeper during her last semester in college. Soon after she graduated, a full-time person who was doing the bookkeeping left very suddenly. Shelli stayed to help out and then decided to stay permanently because she likes being her own boss as well as "being responsible for knowing where the company is financially."

RESPONSIBILITIES. Shelli says that in a larger company she'd probably be called the controller because she handles all of the accounting for the company such as the general ledger, payroll, and accounts payable. She prepares all the monthly financial statements, verifying all the figures and reconciling all internal accounts and bank accounts as she does a monthly reconciliation of the general ledger. She generates all the company's monthly and annual state and federal tax reports; calculates state sales taxes, state and federal payroll taxes, and employee deductions for health insurance and other benefits; and handles all the corporate insurance. Every year she is part of the management team that supervises the annual physical inventory and reconciles the counts with year-end financial records.

On a day-to-day basis, Shelli is responsible for all the money that comes in and is paid out—usually about $100,000 a week— so she makes sure that the cash balances every day. Shelli also is responsible for the company's point-of-sale computer system, which allows her to track margins, sales, and profits on a daily basis. She supervises one full-time employee who does the accounts receivable, data processing of inventory, and filing.

CHALLENGES. One of the most challenging aspects of Shelli's job is managing the cash flow—deciding which bills to pay immediately and which ones to pay a little later. She says managing the finances of a company is "always a balancing act." While the math skills she uses are fairly basic, anyone doing a job like this needs to be good at working with numbers and needs to be willing to give a great deal of attention to detail. Shelli is emphatic when she says there's "lots of room for error if you're not accurate." She likes working with numbers all day; in fact, Shelli says numbers make up at least 80 percent of her job.

Bank Tellers

Bank tellers have more contact with the public than any other bank employees. While many banks have "all-purpose tellers," larger banks often their tellers in more specialized functions, including:

- selling savings bonds,
- accepting utility bill payments,
- receiving Christmas Club deposits,
- managing access to safe deposit boxes,
- recording and completing paperwork for customer loans,
- selling traveler's checks,
- handling and exchanging foreign currency,
- processing certificates of deposit,
- processing money market accounts, and
- computing interest on savings accounts.

In order to handle their responsibilities, tellers need to learn the bank's computer system and be familiar with security procedures. They need to enjoy working with the public. Although tellers need to be comfortable working independently, they also need to realize that their work is closely supervised.

Initial Training

Tellers need both numerical skills and good clerical skills. Virtually all tellers have a high school education, and some also have additional vocational or college training. Many banks provide on-the-job training as well as formal seminars to help new tellers gain familiarity with specialized equipment and the procedures used in that particular bank.

Earning Potential

The most recent edition of the *Occupational Outlook Handbook* reports that the median earnings of full-time bank tellers are $12,800. The lowest 10 percent earn about $9,200; the top 10 percent earn approximately $21,300. The median earnings of supervisors can be as high as approximately $23,700. Many bank tellers as well as supervisors receive a variety of fringe benefits.

In the Workplace as a Bank Teller

Becky Tschantz (pronounced "shots") is a customer service representative at Ames Savings Bank.

BACKGROUND. When Becky graduated from high school, she enrolled in a two-month program at the Teller Training Institute. In very small classes, she received training in many aspects of banking procedures and learned to operate equipment that she might encounter in banks—from those banks still working on manual systems to those that are completely computerized. Becky says that in high school she was only "fair at math, certainly not exceptional," and she thought accounting was easy enough but not very interesting. But she decided to try an entry-level position in banking based on her mother's recommendation. After she completed the Teller Training Institute program, Becky's first job was as a teller for Home Plan Savings and Loan. Then she was invited to apply for a position at American Federal and decided that opportunities for training as well as good benefits made a change appealing. After her training at American Federal, she was transferred to a branch office and given more responsibility and a new teller title: banking services specialist. She worked on new accounts as well as installment and mortgage loans. Ongoing training was a regular part of her job—sessions included number skills (glance at number and remember it), business letter writing, security procedures, cross-selling, and updates about the computer system.

When American Federal was taken over by the Resolution Trust Corporation and then sold, Becky decided to look for a new position. Since coming to Ames Savings Bank, Becky has taken correspondence courses, paid for by the bank, through the Institute of Financial Education. These courses include teller operation, deposit accounts and services, managing deposit accounts and services. With additional training and perhaps five or six more years of experience, Becky hopes to become a savings supervisor.

RESPONSIBILITIES. Becky's primary responsibility is waiting on customers, which involves lots of different tasks. For example, she is responsible for making deposits, withdrawals, and transfers for customers. Another part of her job involves filing records of transactions—signature cards, copies of checks, address changes, and data changes on accounts. She also helps solve customer problems. For example, she not only can help them decide whether a particular bank service is what they need, but she can help customers balance their checking accounts. Recently, she helped a customer decide the best way to take a large amount of cash to Germany. Carrying cash was not an option and the amount was too large for traveler's checks to be a good security choice. After discussing the benefits and problems of several options, Becky advised the customer to carry a bank check that could be changed into German currency upon arrival.

At Ames Savings Bank, each teller has separate responsibilities beyond regular customer service: one credits payments on installment loan accounts, another is in charge of the coin machine, another is designated as the vault teller, and still another is the safe deposit teller. At the end of each day, Becky (and each of the other tellers) is responsible for balancing her cash drawer and checking that the cash and checks she has match what the computer says she has. She verifies the balances of monies received and dispersed and checks the journal (used to record internal transfers) and the general ledger.

JOB APPEAL. Though Becky estimates that only 20 percent of her responsibilities involve quantitative skills, some are a regular part of her job. For instance, she has to be able figure interest rates or penalties on certificates of deposit; make sure deposits are correctly entered; read all customer transactions; and verify monthly totals on new accounts she's opened. The rest of her job she says is, simply, good customer service. In fact, customers are Becky's focus; she says the very best part of her job is "definitely good customers."

Addresses for Further Information

Information about careers as general managers and top executives:

American Management Association
    Management Information Service
    135 West 50th Street
    New York, NY 10020

National Management Association
    2210 Arbor Blvd.
    Dayton, OH 45439

Information about financial management careers:

Financial Executives Institute
    Academic Relations Committee
    P.O. Box 1938
    Morristown, NJ 07962-1938

Information on careers in public administration:

The National Association of Counties
  440 First Street, NW
  Washington, DC 20001

Information about banking occupations and training opportunities:

American Bankers Association
  Reference Librarian
  1120 Connecticut Avenue, NW
  Washington, DC 20036

Institute of Financial Education
  111 E. Wacker Drive
  Chicago, IL 60601

CHAPTER FOUR

Guiding Investments

T his chapter introduces you to professionals who work as much with people as they do with money. For many of them, the people are far more important than the money. Securities and financial services sales representatives make up a large category of professionals who guide investments. But other professionals, such as mortgage officers, see a major part of their job as helping people make appropriate financial investments. Because of the growing array and complexity of financial products and the expanding services offered by many banks, these careers have a strong outlook for the 1990s.

Mortgage Officers

Mortgage officers evaluate, authorize, and recommend or deny loans for real estate. They are responsible for collecting and verifying all the data from a loan applicant to evaluate whether the customer qualifies for a mortgage, and then for recommending the most appropriate kind of loan for that customer.

Initial Training

Bank officers need to be well educated and well informed about economic and financial concepts and trends, so an undergraduate college degree is important. However, these professionals enter the field with a variety of majors.

Earning Potential

The most recent issue of the *Occupational Outlook Handbook* reports that financial managers receive a median annual salary of $32,800. The lowest 10 percent earn $17,500 or less, while the top 10 percent earn more than $52,000. The salary level depends on the size and location of the organization; it's likely to be higher in cities.

In the Workplace as a Mortgage Loan Sales Representative

Kelli Sampson is the mortgage loan sales representative for a branch office of Midland Savings Bank. As the manager of the mortgage department she has four people working for her: a mortgage loan processor, a mortgage loan closer, and two assistants.

BACKGROUND. Kelli has a B.S. in business with a minor in personnel. On her way to becoming head of her branch bank's mortgage department, she previously worked in marketing, as a teller, and as a mortgage loan originator for another bank. She estimates that approximately 35 percent of her job involves quantitative skills, 25 percent involves taking loan applications, 30 percent involves phone communication, and 10 percent involves troubleshooting problems that arise during applications. The majority of the applications she has to deny are for bad credit. For example, when a student misses payments or even defaults on a college loan, that payment history stays on his or her credit record and may prevent him or her from obtaining a mortgage.

RESPONSIBILITIES. Kelli sees her primary responsibilities as offering a variety of mortgage loan programs to customers, making quantitative and qualitative assessments of a customer's ability to handle a particular debt level, and recommending the best match between the customer's ability to pay and the programs available. Kelli typically gets more than 150 mortgage loans approved a year for an average loan of $60,000. Despite this, however, she says her work is "definitely a people business."

CHALLENGES. She recognizes that applying for a mortgage and making a large financial commitment that may last for thirty years is stressful, so she does everything she can to make the process easier and to reduce the stress. For example, when she accepted the position, one of her first decisions was to eliminate the telephone answering machine that gave mortgage rates when people called in; she has human operators—real people who can answer questions for potential customers. She thinks of the people behind the money. For example, she keeps a box of toys for restless children who come with their parents for mortgage interviews, she keeps jelly beans on her desk for treats, and she gives people new to the city a telephone book so they can check available services. On a community level she spearheaded her bank's involvement with the city's affordable housing program that enables first-time home buyers a chance to enter the housing market.

EXPECTATIONS. Kelli's bank is in the process of changing over to a centralized mortgage processing center. The new system will enable Kelli to handle a far higher volume of mortgage loans, in part because the processing and closing will be centralized and in part because the number crunching will be computerized. When she talks about the changes in her department, Kelli stresses the importance of balancing number crunching with human relations.

Securities and Financial Services Sales Representatives

Securities sales representatives have several different job titles: registered representatives, account executives, and brokers, depending on at least two factors. Different companies call the same job by different titles, and titles change as individuals invest increasingly large amounts of money.

Initial Training

Securities sales representatives need to be well educated and well informed about economic and financial concepts and trends, so an undergraduate college degree is important; however, representatives enter the field with a variety of majors. Beyond this, securities sales representatives need to pass a series of exams including a state licensing exam, the Uniform Securities Agents State Law Examination, and the General Securities Registered Representative Examination administered by the National Association of Securities Dealers. In addition, they must submit to an FBI investigation of their background.

Earning Potential

The most recent issue of the *Occupational Outlook Handbook* reports that the Securities Industry Association identifies the average annual earnings of beginning securities sales representatives as $28,000. Full-time experienced securities sales representatives who serve individual investors earn approximately $71,000 a year. Trainees usually receive $1,000 to $1,400 a month until they meet licensing and registration requirements. Earnings depend on commissions from the sale or purchase of stocks and bonds, mutual funds, insurance, or other securities. Financial services sales representatives are paid a salary plus a bonus if they achieve certain goals.

In the Workplace as a Senior Account Executive

Sarah J. Madison will tell you that her job as a senior account executive for Waddell & Reed, one of the country's major financial services, has more to do with people and financial concepts than with money. Despite her job as an account executive, in which she advises people about investing millions of dollars every year, Sally doesn't do number crunching. In fact, if you ask, she'll tell you that she doesn't even really like math. What she does like, though, is helping people understand the implications of various kinds of investments for reaching their long-range goals. She says, "The creative part of this job is problem solving, figuring out how people can reach their goals, given the available dollars they have to invest on a regular basis."

RESPONSIBILITIES.   An important part of Sally's job as a financial planning professional is presenting retirement seminars for employees at one of the country's top computer companies, Digital Equipment Corporation. She introduces long-range planning issues so that people start to think about what they're doing with their retirement dollars. Then when she sits down to develop individual investment plans, she can personalize her recommendations based on a client's needs. This kind of personalized planning begins with collecting data. For example, Sally collects information about the individual's monthly cash flow, long-range objectives (something like sending a child to college or saving for retirement), the time frame for achieving these objectives, and the risk the person is willing to take. During this stage, Sally has to be an active listener, verifying what she hears her client say and checking it with what the person actually does. When she hears a client say he or she wants an aggressive investment program but he has always kept cash reserves in a 4 percent savings account at the bank, she knows that she needs to educate him or her about "aggressive investments" and the risks those investments might involve.

Once the data are collected, Sally can analyze them (using her computer for number crunching). Using this analysis to create a plan that suggests ways the client might reach his or her goals is the creative and conceptual part of her job. Once the plan is implemented, Sally works regularly with each client to review and periodically update the plan, modifying it whenever necessary based on changes in cash flow (for example, she recommends that people have a cash reserve of at least two to six months income), objectives, time frame, and risk.

ONGOING TRAINING. Most organizations offer preliminary training as well as ongoing seminars and mini-courses. Recently, for example, even though Sally is a senior account executive, she attended a seminar about "Investing Distributions from Tax-Qualified Retirement Plans," which suggested additional ways she might assist some of her retired clients. She might have a client take money—perhaps more than $100,000—from a tax-deferred retirement plan such as a 401(k) or 403(b). The client then has sixty days to decide how to invest money as an IRA rollover so he or she can continue to defer the tax. The seminar reviewed changes in the tax laws and suggested a range of investment possibilities for clients with different tolerances for risk.

CHALLENGES. One of the most common planning problems Sally encounters is people who want to save and invest for their children's college education. She has to help them calculate a future education expense based on today's dollars. Typically, college costs increase about 7 percent per year, so if parents of two children, ages six and eight, are willing to invest $5,000 per year for each child for four years of college, that would be $5,000 for two years, then $10,000 for two more years, then back to $5,000 for two final years for a total of $40,000. But it's ten and twelve years before these children will be ready for college. Once her clients have a realistic sense of how much they need to have, they are able to develop a realistic plan for achieving that goal.

In the Workplace as a Financial Advisor

Edward S. Kapron is a financial advisor for Prudential Securities, whose approximately three hundred branches make it one of the top brokerage firms in the country. Even though Ed works in the downtown Pittsburgh office, he has clients in twenty-six states, ranging from Alabama, Alaska, and Arizona to Texas, Vermont, and West Virginia.

BACKGROUND.   Ed came to Prudential Securities with a degree in mechanical engineering and professional experience in technical sales, design engineering, and insurance. When he started to work as a financial advisor, Ed completed a four-month, in-house training course at Prudential Securities to prepare him to pass a required exam so that he could be licensed by the Securities and Exchange Commission (SEC). Because Ed also works with commodities, he has since taken a commodities exam that is required for licensing.

RESPONSIBILITIES.   Ed sees his primary responsibility as helping clients make investments that match their needs and investment objectives. He determines this suitability by talking with clients about things such as their financial plans, their goals, their willingness to take financial risks, and the length of time they want the investment to last. Because clients need to understand what each specific investment can do for them, Ed's job involves teaching—helping his clients to understand their investment options and to evaluate the benefits of each option before they settle on an investment plan.

REQUIREMENTS.   Ed's job requires a combination of communication skills such as reading, writing, listening, and speaking; as well as interpersonal skills, sales skills, and financial know-how. He explains that an important part of his job involves "reading information to assess the performance and potential of a company." He has two broad ways to analyze the information he collects. When Ed uses a *fundamental analysis,* he looks at factors such as a company's earnings, sales, and management, which is helpful for clients who want long-term investment (at least eighteen months or more). When Ed uses a *technical analysis,* he refers to a chart that shows trends (thirty-day trends as well as two hundred-day trends) in a company's price, which is helpful for clients who want short-term investments (usually fewer than twelve months). The math skills Ed uses in his job are fairly basic. Although he doesn't use the theoretical and complex engineering math that he took as part of his degree, he says that his background "skill and comfort in knowing numbers lets me transform and use concepts."

TECHNOLOGY. To help him evaluate investment alternatives, Ed has access to a networked computer terminal, which gives him up-to-the-second prices from the New York Stock Exchange and the Chicago Board of Trade. He uses this terminal to retrieve his clients' portfolios so that when he talks with a client, he can provide updated information. Like most financial advisors, Ed sees the second computer on his desk—an individual personal computer—as a critical marketing tool that he uses (1) to generate graphics to compare performance of mutual funds, (2) to store and retrieve information, and (3) to design newsletters sent to clients.

EARNINGS. During a typical year, Ed usually handles about $13 million in investments, which generate about $150,000-$200,000 in commissions. Ed earns approximately 30 percent of these commissions. When Ed's commissions increase, his percentage of those commissions also will increase; he can anticipate earning approximately 40 percent of gross commissions exceeding $250,000.

In the Workplace as a Credit Counselor

Dale Rahfeldt, a registered investment advisor and certified financial planner, provides clients with financial planning, investment assistance, and debt counseling.

BACKGROUND. Dale has a B.S. in sociology, with minors in philosophy and psychology. His work experience is separated into four chunks: sales, corporate training, personnel management, and financial planning and counseling. He first spent time working as a sales representative and as a sales manager. Later he worked for twelve years as a sales rep and developer for training programs in International Correspondence Schools' Industrial Training Division. He conducted training for companies such as Inland Steel, Johnson & Johnson, Reynolds Metals, and Interlake Steel. After that, he spent a year as the in-house trainer for management development and supervision at Oak Forest Hospital in Chicago. Then he spent two years as director of personnel for Aurora Metal Company, followed by four years as the supervisor of technical training for Sundstrand. Most recently, he spent eight years as a registered representative for IDS Financial Services. Five years ago, he started his own business.

RESPONSIBILITIES.   Dale spends about 40 percent of his time helping his clients establish or identify financial goals and considering ways to accomplish these goals. He spends another 25 percent of his time advising people about investments.

The final 35 percent of his time is spent doing debt counseling with clients who have serious financial problems, which is the focus of his work described in this book. First, he has to find out what kind of financial trouble his clients are in. Then he has to find out how they got into that trouble. Finally, he works with his clients to develop a plan to get out of the current problems and prevent them from happening in the future.

CHALLENGES.   Dale says that his background in personnel management, industrial training, and financial investments is useful, but a great deal of what he helps clients with is applying lots of common sense to their problems. For example, he says that many clients with serious debt problems need to learn to do the following things:

- keep records;
- balance their checkbook;
- identify how much interest they're paying on credit cards and loans . . . and know how that translates into dollars;

- recognize when they are in danger of overextending;
- understand comparable value and comparison shopping (on everything from T-shirts to cars);
- understand the concept of finance charges (Dale says he tells some clients that if they'd paid cash for their cars instead of using their method of financing, they'd get every third car virtually for free);
- ask questions that encourage full disclosure;
- be able to recognize when key information about financing is missing;
- distinguish between "need" and "want"; and
- not allow themselves to be harassed by creditors.

Dale says many people get into financial difficulty because they overspend based on their immediately available cash—without thinking about other upcoming expenses. Then they compound the problem by paying the creditors who "yell the loudest" and ignoring the others. He says that by the time most people come to him, they have serious credit card and tax problems (for example, having their wages garnished or receiving an IRS assessment for their paycheck).

Many of these people don't know where to turn. They listen to an ad on the television and decide to consolidate debts, which results in a high interest charge. And worse, for some people, debt consolidation can create additional problems because they have the sense that they now have extra money.

Debts can be managed in a number of ways. Some debt management companies take the client's paycheck, pay the bills, give the client an allowance, and take a fee based on the amount of dollars distributed. Other organizations, usually employed and paid by credit card companies, help clients distribute regular payments to creditors. Unfortunately, these approaches seldom include any education or financial planning to help the client prevent financial problems in the future. Dale charges a very small flat fee for eighteen months of debt counseling (possible because he has income from other parts of his business) and then meets frequently with clients to go through bills and jointly identify ways to meet the financial obligations. Dale helps clients see options and tries to convince them not to make unreasonable commitments to creditors. For example, a creditor may want $80 a month, but the client can only afford $10 a month. Dale helps the client communicate with the creditor and not be bullied into paying more than he or she can manage. He then urges his clients to be consistent in meeting the commitments they've agreed to.

Dale says his goal is for clients to be able to manage independently and prevent future problems, to develop a plan for savings, and eventually to be able to manage financial and estate planning and investment.

Buying in the Workplace

B uying in the workplace comes in many forms. This chapter focuses on professionals who buy for retail businesses. These are generally fast-paced, highly competitive jobs with lots of hours and lots of pressure.

Buyers

Buyers for retail stores are shoppers, only on a large scale. They purchase merchandise—from household goods and clothing to electronic components and machinery—for resale. Buyers fall into two broad categories:

- *Wholesale buyers* purchase goods directly from manufacturers or other wholesale firms for resale to retail firms or to other commercial organizations.
- *Retail buyers* purchase goods from wholesale firms or directly from manufacturers for resale to the public.

Not only do buyers try to obtain the best available merchandise for the lowest possible price, they also work with sales and marketing managers to determine how the merchandise will be distributed and marketed. Buyers working for medium-sized and large companies usually specialize in purchasing one or two lines of merchandise, whereas buyers working for small stores may purchase the entire stock of merchandise.

Initial Training

The route to becoming a buyer varies from company to company. Some firms promote qualified employees to assistant buyer positions; others recruit and train college graduates and other applicants. Most stores prefer applicants who have completed associate degree or bachelor degree programs in fields such as marketing or purchasing. Most buyers begin as trainees before they are promoted to assistant buyers and, eventually, to buyers. Trainee programs usually combine classroom instruction in merchandising and purchasing coupled with short job rotations in areas such as sales, accounts receivable, and the stock room. Even after becoming a buyer, professionals in the field often take courses in merchandising techniques, attend trade shows and conferences, and read industry publications.

Earning Potential

The most recent edition of the *Occupational Outlook Handbook* reports that the median income for buyers is $24,700. Most buyers earn between $17,500 and $35,500 a year. The lowest 10 percent average less than $14,000; the top 10 percent earn more than $45,500. Higher salaries are more likely in large organizations and vary somewhat according to factors such as the amount and type of product purchased and the employer's sales volume. Buyers for large wholesale distributors and for mass merchandisers such as large discount or chain department stores are among the most highly paid.

In the Workplace as a Retail Buyer

Sam Shaver is the decorative housewares buyer for Younkers Department Stores, a 28-store corporation throughout the Midwest with headquarters in Iowa. Sam travels overseas for what he considers the most exciting part of his job—negotiating with overseas vendors for the design, manufacture, and shipment of decorative housewares, which include dinnerware, glassware, acrylics, wood, and ceramics. As part of these negotiations, Sam must reach agreements with the vendors about things such as the designs they will undertake; the minimum quantities they're willing to manufacture; the design, quantity, and price of boxing; and delivery dates. This travel usually means going to Taiwan, but it sometimes means the Philippines or Hong Kong.

BACKGROUND. More than twenty years ago, after two years of college, Sam started as a trainee—the usual place for buyers to begin—for D. H. Holmes, at that time a full-line department store in New Orleans. After a year as a trainee in operations (which included the warehouse function of a department store), Sam was promoted to superintendent of the warehouse for the home area of twenty-two stores, which collectively had an annual sales volume of approximately $24 million. After five years, Sam followed a typical career path when he transferred to the merchandise division of D. H. Holmes where he worked as a store manager for one of their small stores—about 30,000 square feet with an annual volume of $6 million—that specialized in home goods. Although most store managers are not involved in buying, Sam was, so he had an easy move when, four years later, he was promoted to a buyer in housewares. That division, with an annual volume of approximately $5 million, was responsible for both basic and decorative housewares. When Dillard's bought D. H. Holmes in 1989, Sam worked as a merchandise manager in one of Dillard's New Orleans stores before accepting a position as decorative housewares buyer for Younkers.

RESPONSIBILITIES. Sam has a wide range of responsibilities; he estimates that about 60 percent of his job involves quantitative elements. Most important, he is responsible for forecasting sales, turnovers, markdowns, and gross margins for six-month periods (spring season and fall season) for a department that averages between $3.5 and $5 million in sales (the total for decorative housewares in all twenty-eight stores). Everything from dips in the regional economy to local upsurges in buying causes Sam to periodically reassess his forecast and consider increasing or reducing orders for particular items. Sam assesses the success of his forecast by examining the breakdown of sales and stock levels by store. To help him with this assessment, he receives a computer printout for decorative housewares in each store from Younkers' mainframe computer (a daily printout for sales; a weekly printout for items on hand, units of stock sold, and stock by classification such as dinnerware, glassware, flatware, wood, and ceramics). The task is complicated as stores differ in the sales forecast for every classification because of factors such as location and competition.

If Sam misjudges, he has merchandise that doesn't sell and has to make a decision about a markdown price, trying to avoid a loss for that particular item. He also is responsible for setting sales goals for each six-month period, for purchasing goods for resale at the best price to achieve his sales goals, and for negotiating with vendors for advertising dollars. Another part of Sam's job is regular communication with all Younkers stores about sales promotions, new merchandise, and new display concepts in decorative housewares.

NEGOTIATION. Younkers is a member of the Frederick Atkins buying group, which has thirty-two member stores. The purpose of a buying group is to get better prices because of volume purchases. When Sam goes to Taiwan, he may take a sketch for a ceramic mug, for example, and get quotations for the design and manufacture of, say, 3,000 units, 10,000 units, and 20,000 units; the greater the volume, the lower the price he can negotiate. Domestic vendors offer less opportunity for negotiating price. However, there is still quite a range that Sam can negotiate for a vendor's contribution to advertising, from as little as 3 percent to as high as 20 percent, based on factors such as volume of sales and anticipated future sales. Once Sam knows the cost of the item itself, he has to add in freight (usually 3 to 6 percent for wood and ceramics, and 8 to 12 percent for glass) and the cost of advertising above the vendor contribution. After that, he can determine the retail markup.

PREPARATION. Although developing expertise in retail buying depends more on on-the-job experience than it does on academic preparation, Sam has found some of his college courses useful, especially those in interior design, communication skills, and time management. However, he says there's ongoing informal training and support provided by divisional merchandise managers (who were typically buyers before their promotion). For someone planning a career in the retail industry, Sam stresses the value of courses in math, accounting, computer applications, and management because activities in these areas make up the majority of his work.

In the Workplace as a Buyer Trainee

Lauri Platter works as a buyer trainee for Fareway Stores, Inc., a chain of fifty-five grocery stores. Each store buys its own chips, beer, soda, snacks, and breads from individual vendors, but the seven buyers in the corporation's centralized buying department are responsible for supplying everything else. Generally, buyers for grocery stores separate items into the following categories:

- refrigerated foods,
- frozen foods,
- health and beauty,
- fresh meat,
- processed and frozen meat,
- produce, and
- groceries, which include virtually everything else. Examples of groceries are flour, sugar, mixes, cereals and related items, canned goods, paper goods, spices, soaps, pickles, condiments, candy, pet items, baby items, coffee, packaged foods, and so forth.

The larger the chain of grocery stores is, the greater the specialization among the buyers. A very large chain might have a buyer who deals primarily with frozen foods or pet items or paper goods. Although the buyers at Fareway do specialize, they have several areas of specialization. For example, one buyer handles all the meat whether fresh, frozen, or processed. And Lauri, as a buyer trainee, handles pet items, baby items, coffee, and some packaged foods (for example, rice, noodles, puddings, and gelatin).

BACKGROUND. Lauri has worked for Fareway Stores in the buying department for thirteen years, so she knows the organization well. However, she's only been a buyer trainee for six months. Immediately after graduating from high school where she took courses in typing, bookkeeping, and math, Lauri went to work as a secretary for a vending machine company. Then she took time off to stay at home with her children. Several years later, after a six-month stint as a part-time clerk, she went to work as a three-day-a-week secretary for the buying department for Fareway, a position she held for ten years. Two years ago, she increased her time to four days a week when the department needed her to become familiar with their new computer system. Six months ago, a buyer position opened up; the head of the department, Bob Carper, asked Lauri if she'd like to become a buyer. When she said yes, he created a buyer trainee position.

RESPONSIBILITIES. Lauri sees herself as having two primary responsibilities: purchasing goods at the lowest possible price and keeping inventory on hand so stores can order from the warehouse. Lauri has several ways she goes about getting the best prices. One way involves responding to special limited-time offers from wholesalers who promote cents-off prices for cases of particular items. Another way is to look for deals where manufacturers are offering specific promotions (for example, a price break, sometimes coupled with financial assistance on advertising, depending on the volume ordered). A third way is to get to know the brokers for different products; they become a valuable resource for cluing buyers in to good prices. Lauri also checks freight rates, knowing that unnecessary freight charges add to the prices consumers have to pay. Finally, she purchases in bulk, by the truckload. Recently, for example, she has ordered a truckload of pet food (44,000 pounds), a truckload of baby foods, a truckload of soups, and a truckload of kitty litter.

Lauri's second responsibility is keeping inventory on hand. She regularly checks the computerized inventory that the warehouse keeps. Items enter the inventory when they arrive at the warehouse and are removed when they're loaded for delivery to individual stores. Lauri works on a "weekly turn" (what's sold in a week plus the delivery time). When stores run ads about specials, Lauri has to calculate that more of the advertised item will be sold during that week than when the item isn't advertised and/or isn't on special. Although individual stores let the warehouse know how much of a special item they plan to order, Lauri says experience is her biggest help in judging inventory levels of her stock. As she's watching stock levels, she also needs to calculate the amount of time she needs to get the order in so the warehouse doesn't run out of the product. For example, when 25-pound bags of a brand name dog food are advertised as a special promotion, they're a fast-moving item. Fareway stores can go through four truckloads of dog food in one week. (That's 176,000 pounds of dog food, more than 7,000 25-pound bags.) A final way that Lauri manages her inventory is by not ordering too much ahead so that stock doesn't get old or outdated. For example, baby foods and formulas have a short shelf life. By ordering smaller shipments, Lauri can plan that these items don't sit in the warehouse for more than two or three weeks.

PREPARATION. Lauri says that when she started she'd already learned about Fareway's computer system that tracks virtually all warehouse information for all items—price, special deals and price breaks, layers and quantity per pallet, cases per pallet, location of pallets, size and weight, weekly and quarterly sales, page listing in store catalog, and buyer. What she needed to learn was how to work with the promotions that were offered so that she could come up with the best price to pass on to customers.

To do her job, Lauri says a person needs a "good attitude and good math ability." You also have to be comfortable with computers and be able to be effective in one-on-one work with a great many people. Lauri says that she has received "lots of help" from Bob Carper and the rest of the buyers. "There's always someone to answer a question." After six months on the job, Lauri is "starting to feel some confidence."

Purchasing Agents

Purchasing agents (purchasing managers, contract managers, procurement officers, industrial buyers) are responsible for obtaining the goods, materials, supplies, and services for their organization. They check the quality as well as the quantity and negotiate the price and the delivery date. Making sure the necessary materials are available is critical for any production process.

- *Purchasing agents* are usually responsible for routine purchases for an organization and often specialize in a group of related commodities such as electronic components, lumber, or livestock.
- *Purchasing managers* are usually responsible for more complex purchasing tasks and may supervise a group of agents handling a number of related goods and services.

Initial Training

Most companies like entry-level purchasing agents to have a college degree or a combination of college courses and work experience. Some companies will hire people without a college degree and have them start as a clerk-buyer and then move up to buyer. However, advancement almost always requires a bachelor's degree and often a master's degree in business. Companies that deal with highly specialized or technical products such as chemicals or machine tools expect purchasing agents to have a technical background. Because so much work is done on the computer, familiarity with computers is very important. Beginning purchasing agents often begin in a training program in order to learn the company's operations and purchasing procedures; then they work with experienced purchasing agents to learn about commodities, prices, suppliers, and negotiating techniques.

The recognized mark of experience and professional competence is the designation Certified Purchasing Manager, conferred by the National Association of Purchasing Management (NAPM). In order to receive this designation, candidates must pass four exams and meet educational and experience requirements. Other designations of professional competence are also possible. State and local government employees who meet experience requirements can pass exams to earn the designation of Professional Public Buyer (PPB) or Certified Public Purchasing Officer (CPPO). Agents specializing in contractual aspects of purchasing and meeting educational and experience requirements can complete advanced coursework and pass exams to earn the designation of Certified Associate Contract Manager (CACM) or Certified Professional Contract Manager (CPCM).

Earning Potential

The most recent edition of the *Occupational Outlook Handbook* reports that the median income for purchasing agents is approximately $25,900. The middle 50 percent of purchasing agents earn between $19,500 and $35,000 a year. The lowest 10 percent average less than $12,000; the top 10 percent earn more than $47,000. The middle 50 percent of purchasing managers earn between $26,000 and $50,000 a year.

In the Workplace as a Purchasing Agent/Manager

Merle Brendeland is the purchasing manager for Sauer-Sundstrand Company, an international corporation that manufactures components for fluid power equipment. The division Merle works for manufactures hydrostatic transmissions, which convert fluid power to wheels for everything from riding lawnmowers to large earth-moving equipment. This division has three locations and one thousand employees, with about $125 million in gross sales and $43 to $44 million in annual purchasing.

JOB DESCRIPTION. The eight purchasing agents whom Merle supervises are the "shoppers for the company," and their primary responsibility is to keep production in operation. At Sauer-Sundstrand, they need to ensure that there are sufficient amounts of the following items:

- raw materials and piece parts (for example, steel, bearings, castings, stampings, laser-cut parts, and so on);
- products (for example, software and leased autos); and
- necessary services (everything from janitorial service and temporary labor to lawn maintenance and pest control).

The purchasing department is responsible for writing all requests for proposals and negotiating all contracts.

These purchasing agents spend about 60 to 70 percent of their time purchasing raw materials and the remainder of their time on what they call MRO—maintenance, repairs, and operations. The purchasing agents tend to specialize in various areas; the company promotes this specialization. For example, purchasing agents are encouraged to learn about the technologies they deal with, the industry leaders, the location of raw materials, and various geopolitical factors that might influence delivery of those materials. Merle explains that it takes two to three years for new purchasing agents to learn "purchasing basics and then to refine their product knowledge from the basics. As they gain experience, they learn a lot about plain old business sense."

BACKGROUND. Merle himself started out with a bachelor's degree in public service administration. His first job was as a buyer in agricultural chemicals. Then he spent thirteen years as the purchasing manager for worldwide purchases for Bourns, an electronics firm in California. Two years ago he came to Sauer-Sundstrand as their purchasing manager. Along the way, he has taken graduate courses focusing on marketing and corporate ethics and responsibility.

RESPONSIBILITIES.   Merle says he now spends little of his time buying. Instead, he spends approximately 40 to 50 percent of his time traveling—visiting vendors, attending trade shows (which he points out are an excellent source of information about new products and services), and visiting other Sauer-Sundstrand facilities. Typically, he makes short trips all over the United States, but he also has done a great deal of overseas travel with trips to the Pacific Rim, Central America, and Europe. Another 20 to 30 percent of his time is spent in negotiations when contracts are over $100,000. In these cases, he works with the Sauer-Sundstrand purchasing agent and the outside vendor. The balance of his time is spent with various administrative tasks and meetings.

Merle explains that most interactions are straightforward, professional arrangements. The purchasing agent and the vendor both understand the "rules." However, he says there are sometimes some unusual situations that make the job unexpectedly interesting. For instance, once a software company tried to predate a major purchase agreement after it had declared bankruptcy; Merle ended up making a deposition in front of the Securities and Exchange Commission (SEC) before the software company recanted its initial claim. Less serious, Merle says, has been trying to understand the price structure and services used by some pest exterminators: what pests are they going to eliminate, how often will they inspect, what guarantees will they make. Or take the case where the local police department wanted the names of the personnel employed by Sauer-Sunstrand's janitorial and trash-hauling contractors. Or the case of the foreign manufacturer who wanted a bonus to guarantee that he used high-quality material and provided uninterrupted work (what he called an "antilabor interruption service"). Or the foreign manufacturer who needed Sauer-Sundstrand to pay the electricity bill (in cash) before work could proceed.

Large contracts for major products are usually for three to five years, so in making decisions about which vendors to use, Merle examines a number of factors. First and most important, he considers the *quality* of the product or service. Along with quality, he considers questions such as whether the company is similar to Sauer-Sundstrand—for example, does it have the same management philosophy? Is it a financially viable organization? Is the management accessible? Can the company handle the job? Then Merle considers *cost*, which involves a great many more factors than the price of the item itself, such as:

- freight;
- ease of use (for example, are the parts in plastic sleeves so that they're time-consuming to get out and use);
- packaging (for example, does it sufficiently protect the product or is it bulky to store);
- cleanliness (for example, do the parts need to be washed before they're used); and
- value added (for example, is steel cut and sorted to length).

Finally, Merle has to consider *delivery*, which includes not only the timeliness of the delivery but whether the vendor is willing to deliver in, say, weekly increments instead of ship once a quarter, which necessitates warehousing or storage.

OBSERVATIONS. Merle believes that purchasing agents are an "undernoticed profession," a profession that is growing in importance as companies seek more and more goods and services from external vendors. As maintaining a vertically integrated industry is becoming prohibitively expensive, the role of purchasing agent is becoming more important. "You don't make money when you sell; you make it on how you buy."

Address for Further Information

National Retail Merchants Association
100 West 31st Street
New York, NY 10001

CHAPTER SIX

Marketing and Selling in the Workplace

Selling is big business, and this chapter can deal only with a few of the many occupations that involve sales. For instance you can work in wholesale or retail sales, you can work directly with the public or you can work in management, or you can sell products or services. Whatever your focus, if you decide to work in sales, you need to have good people skills and good problem-solving skills. You also need to be able to be persuasive and good-natured in the face of unexpected conflicts.

Sales Service Representatives

Sales service representatives sell a wide variety of services, from linen supplies to cable TV, from educational services to telephone communication systems. Some sales service representatives sell complex services such as inventory control, payroll processing, sales analysis, and financial reporting. Several examples illustrate the possibilities:

- An educational sales service representative might persuade states to use a particular licensing exam on insurance laws and regulations.

- A hotel sales service representative could contact government, business, and professional groups to solicit convention and conference business for the hotel.
- Fund-raisers plan programs to raise money for charities or other causes such as the Special Olympics.
- Sales service representatives for temporary help agencies can locate and acquire clients who will use the company's services.
- Telephone sales service representatives contact and visit commercial customers to review their communication system, analyze their communication needs, and recommend appropriate equipment and services to meet those needs.

Despite the diversity of the services, all sales service representatives share a number of characteristics. They all must understand and be able to explain their company's service. The procedures they follow are similar in that they develop lists of prospective clients to contact. They select from a variety of methods—discussions, demonstrations, audiovisual presentations, reading material, question-and-answer sessions—to try to persuade the potential customer to purchase the service. If the potential customer buys the service, the sales service representative regularly follows up to make sure that the service is meeting the customer's needs.

Initial Training

Most sales service representatives have a college degree. Employers who have a complex or technical service may require that their sales service representatives have specialized degrees in marketing, computer silence, or engineering. Many companies have their own training program that introduces the company's operations and services as well as reviews various sales techniques such as prospecting for customers, probing customer needs, interviewing, sales presentations, and closing a sale. Some companies also provide motivational and sensitivity training.

Earning Potential

According to the most recent *Occupational Outlook Handbook,* the median annual earnings for specialized sales service representatives are $23,700. Earnings of sales service representatives are considerably higher for those who sell technical services such as computer or communication services. Some sales service representatives can earn over $100,000 a year.

In the Workplace as an Account Representative for a Telecommunications Company

Lisa Ettlinger is a senior major account representative for MCI, a telecommunications company. When Lisa started at MCI seven years ago, the company had 450 employees; now it has 25,000, which means that employees not only have lots of opportunities, but they also need to be flexible and adapt to the many changes that are part of a rapidly growing company.

MAJOR ACCOUNTS. Lisa's own professional success has paralleled the success of MCI. She started out in telemarketing and then was promoted to account executive (level 1) in general business sales. After that she moved up to a position as senior account executive (level 1) and then to account executive (level 2). Another promotion brought her to senior account executive (level 2) and another one to her current position as senior major account representative. Lisa's commitment to her job at MCI is rewarded. She works on a salary plus commission basis, with approximately 50 percent of her income coming from each. For people in her position, the base salary ranges between $30,000 to $50,000, with no ceiling on commissions.

In order to be considered as a major account by MCI, a company needs to have long-distance telephone expenses ranging from approximately $50,000/month to $400,000/month. (Above that amount, the accounts are handled by a national account representative.) Typically Lisa manages a dozen major accounts, counting among her clients well-known firms in finance, retail business, computer software, medicine, and photoimaging. She says this variety is one of the best parts of her job.

BACKGROUND. Lisa says her job is essentially a sales position, so her bachelor's degree in psychology with a minor in public relations helps her deal with different people in different environments. She gets to use theories of human behavior everyday.

Lisa also acknowledges the value of her background in math. She says she's lucky to have mathematical aptitude so that working with numbers is interesting and easy. These quantitative skills come in handy when she's dealing with customers who have strong quantitative backgrounds. For example, people she regularly works with at two of her current major accounts expect her to be comfortable using quantitative concepts (and vocabulary) to explore their companies' telecommunication needs.

Lisa knows that courses she's taken in calculus, basic geometry, and computer science have been helpful especially since a good deal of her job requires her to analyze complex financial statements and write proposals for new major accounts, which she says "have lots of numbers." Included in a proposal is a detailed estimate of all the costs involved with the MCI services a company would use. This cost estimate includes a different rate structure for every service or product, a structure that is affected by a large number of variables, some of which are time of service (day/evening/night), geographic ranges, and volume discounts. Lisa needs the ability to conceptualize a major proposal, which includes projections of the payback period for different configurations of services as well as monthly and annual expenses and savings. Although Lisa has computers to help her do many of the estimates and projections, they don't do everything, so her quantitative skills are important.

RESPONSIBILITIES. Lisa separates her responsibilities into two broad categories: managing existing accounts and pursuing new accounts. Her responsibilities to her customers start with knowing how their business works so she can make sure that they have the technology for the services they need; that their network is operating correctly; and that they are aware of new products that might make their work more efficient or convenient.

Lisa explains that one of the most important aspects of getting new accounts is doing research to understand as much as possible about how their business works. So, for example, when she recently was working to add a major trauma center to her list of accounts, she not only learned about their business operations and telecommunications, but she also learned about the special needs they had because of their medical specialty. Part of her job in selling involves making customers aware of the many services they can use with MCI—services for data transmission, lines for video conferencing, conference calling, phone mail, and FAX services, for example. Depending on which of the sixty-nine products/services she's focusing on, Lisa may contact people in telecommunications, finance, or marketing.

In learning about her customers, Lisa reads a great deal about business in the *Wall Street Journal,* trade magazines, and annual reports. She also takes MCI training classes, which are offered regularly on a variety of topics including all sixty-nine MCI products as well as training in sales, management, communications, time-management, and data services.

Retail Sales

Because retail sales is a highly competitive business, and retail sales workers have more contact with customers than any other employees in the business, it's important that these workers create a positive impression on the customers. Increasingly, employers are stressing the importance of customer service and satisfaction.

Retail sales workers' primary responsibility is to interest customers in the merchandise. To do this, they need to be personable, but equally important, they need to know about the merchandise, its construction, quality, features, and models. Retail sales workers also have to be knowledgeable about security procedures. For some jobs, retail sales workers need to have specialized knowledge—for example, sales of personal computers, electronic entertainment (VCRs, CD players, etc.), lumber, appliances, and garden/yard fertilizers and pesticides.

In addition to selling merchandise, retail sales workers are often expected to complete a variety of tasks, including the following:

• open and close the cash register,
• handle cash, check, and charge payments,
• make out sales slips,
• handle returns and exchanges,
• make deposits in the cash office,
• help stock shelves and racks,
• take inventory, and
• prepare displays.

In some stores, customer satisfaction is so important that retail sales workers are encouraged to help customers locate what they need, even if it means suggesting other stores the customer might try.

Initial Training

Most retail sales positions have no formal education requirements. However, sales workers must enjoy working with people, be tactful, and make a positive impression. Most small organizations have informal on-the-job training, with the manager or a more experienced employee showing the new sales worker the procedures. Larger organizations sometimes have more formal training programs. These programs can take the form of several days of orientation, including presentations, demonstrations, video training tapes, and hands-on practice. Subjects covered usually include making cash, check, and charge sales; customer service; returns and exchanges; store security; and store policies.

Earning Potential

Earnings of retail sales workers vary tremendously by the type of business, the product being sold, and the employee's experience. Some businesses start retail sales workers at minimum wage. (Employees under age twenty can be paid a lower "training wage" for up to six months.) Some retail sales workers receive a salary plus commission; others work on a salary-only or a commission-only basis. Benefits usually depend on the size of the business.

According to the most recent *Occupational Outlook Handbook*, these are typical average weekly earnings for entry-level retail sales workers, differentiated by type of goods sold:

motor vehicles and boats	$439
furniture and home furnishings	354
auto, electronic, and other parts	323
radio, television, stereo, and appliances	322
door-to-door item sales	302
hardware and building supplies	300
apparel	207
other commodities	217

In the Workplace in Retail Lumber Sales

Lee Foster works in contractor and retail lumber sales for Chagnon Lumber and Home Center. He's been there for a year. Before that he worked for Webber Lumber for six years, most recently as a manager (promoted from assistant manager and salesman). Prior to that, he worked for five years for Grossman's as an area supervisor (promoted from salesman and stockboy). Chagnon Lumber and Home Center has annual sales of about $10 million. The company currently employs about twenty salespeople. The industry is keyed on the local and regional economy, so in better economic times Chagnon has up to fifty employees with annual sales of $50 million.

RESPONSIBILITIES. Lee's primary responsibility, in fact about 60 percent of his job, involves selling materials to contractors. In order to do this well, he needs extensive product knowledge so that he can recommend which products to use in specific situations. For example, he needs to know about the strength factor of using 2-inch x 6-inch lumber versus 2-inch x 10-inch lumber. He needs to know how various species of lumber such as pine, oak, and mahogany differ in appearance, strength, practicality, and durability. He needs to know features and functions of different brands of doors and windows—insulating value, upkeep, air infiltration. Another 25 percent of Lee's responsibilities involve handling special order purchasing. The final 15 percent of his responsibilities involve doing material take-off's from blueprints. For example, a contractor brings in blueprints, and Lee gives the contractor a list of all materials needed for the building.

Lee has twelve years of experience in retail lumber sales. This background enables him to know where to get what. He knows what product will fit a particular need and what suppliers to contact. Although virtually anything is available for a certain cost, Lee likes to present customers with options, so he works to recommend the most appropriate product for the least cost and does a cost-benefit analysis of additional features. For example, a customer who needs fascia boards (trim boards) may want them in redwood; Lee then will explain that pine fascia boards are also an option. Although pine doesn't have insect or rot resistance, it is available at one-third the cost. Similarly, Lee knows various distributors who handle a standard item with the same specs (the same hollow-core door can be $12 from one distributor and $20 from another distributor).

APPLIED MATH. After two and one-half years of college in business management, Lee went into retail lumber sales. He says his college courses were useful in teaching him how to deal with people. They also were useful in giving him a foundation in math, which is very important in his job. Lee says that he uses everything up to calculus on a daily basis. Typically, he may have to figure the angle of a roof (its pitch) or may have to figure the amount of lumber necessary to construct special-order windows that have unusual geometric shapes. Even after he started working at lumber yards, Lee kept taking job-related seminars in a variety of topics, from the limitations of various window designs to pricing schedules for window applications.

Lee estimates that at least 70 percent of his job directly involves basic math. He says, "It seems like I use numbers every minute of every day because basically I'm working with money, which is numbers." For example, handling special orders involves taking the wholesale cost and converting it into a sales price by considering markup (difference between the selling price and the cost) and margin (profitability, including overhead). Lee could buy a basic steel door for $100. With a 45 percent markup, he could sell it for $145; that would give him a margin of, say, 29 percent, after he takes handling and overhead into account. Or he could buy a custom-sized door for $100 and sell it to customer for $175; the markup would be 75 percent, but the margin might be 50 percent after he takes handling and overhead into account. The markup, which varies depending on the product, its features, and the customer, can range from 18 percent to 300 percent; however, a typical markup is about 40 percent.

SUGGESTIONS. Lee suggests that anyone interested in going into retail sales take courses in business; math, such as algebra, trigonometry, geometry, and basic calculus; and management. But the key, he says, is experience. "It's vital to have experience; it makes the difference between someone who takes orders and someone who fulfills customers needs."

Marketing

The fundamental objective of any organization is to market its products or services profitably. In very small companies, the owner may assume all marketing responsibilities. In large companies, an experienced marketing manager coordinates these efforts. This manager is generally responsible for the overall marketing policy, which may include the following activities:

- conducting market research to determine the demand for the products and/or services,
- monitoring trends that indicate need for new products and services,
- developing pricing strategies,
- overseeing product development,
- developing a marketing strategy to promote the firm's products and services, and
- working cooperatively with sales, advertising, and public relations to implement the marketing strategies.

Initial Training

A wide range of backgrounds are suitable for entry into marketing, but many employers prefer a broad liberal arts background. Some employers prefer that people in marketing management have a bachelor's degree or a master's degree in business administration with a concentration in marketing. Coursework in business law, economics, accounting, finance, mathematics, and statistics is also highly recommended. In highly technical industries, a bachelor's degree in engineering, computer science, or science coupled with a master's degree in marketing is preferred.

Earning Potential

According to the most recent *Occupational Outlook Handbook*, the median annual income for marketing managers is $36,500. The lowest 10 percent earn $19,200 or less, while the top 10 percent earn more than $52,000. Salaries between $75,000 and $100,000 are not uncommon. Salaries vary substantially depending on the level of managerial responsibility, length of service, and size and location of the organization.

In the Workplace as a Marketing Research Manager

Dale Keever is the marketing research manager for the Iowa Lottery.

BACKGROUND. Dale came to the Lottery Commission with an associate's degree in accounting. Since then he has earned a bachelor's degree in management with a minor in computer science. He believes continuing education is important so he regularly enrolls in one or two seminars every year. For example, he went to Notre Dame's school of marketing research for a one-week seminar. Before he came to the Lottery, he worked as a budgeting analyst with Iowa's Department of Human Services.

RESPONSIBILITIES. One of Dale's primary responsibilities is cre- ating and maintaining historical and demographical databases about the lottery that are available to the director of the lottery as well as other employees in, for example, sales and marketing. Dale needs to analyze their needs for the data and organize the information in a way that anticipates their questions. Quite simply, he sees himself "as a repository of information that people can use."

Dale also is involved in new product development. When ideas for new lottery products come to Dale for evaluation, he computes the odds of winning and builds computer models that consider many different variables. Then he takes these models and does qualitative research with focus groups and quantitative research in which he analyzes a number of elements: What's the potential market share? Will they cannibalize their own games? Are there differences in play behavior between men and women? Are there critical geographic factors to consider such as state border or rural/urban customers? Another responsibility Dale has involves defining marketing strategies for the team that writes the marketing plans for each year. He also evaluates promotional and advertising activities using several different methodologies, including external, contracted marketing projects, and internal projects. Sometimes he acts as a project manager for internal projects, keeping track of factors such as cost effectiveness and turn-around time.

CHALLENGES. In explaining some of the problems that he works on, Dale talks about using a technique called conjoint analysis to identify attributes people want in new lottery products as well as to modify features of existing lottery games. To use this technique, Dale takes a lottery product and lists its attributes. Respondents then order these attributes by rank. The respondents' rank ordering is used to reorder attributes so that the most popular ones are listed first. In using conjoint analysis to develop a new game, the Iowa Lotto with Wild Card, Dale used a sample of four hundred respondents who rank ordered the potential attributes via a computer-aided interviewing process. Later, these respondents played a trial version of the new game and then were interviewed about preferences and problems.

SUGGESTIONS. Dale explains that analytical skills are very useful, in fact essential to marketing research. A marketing research analyst spends about 80 percent of the time in analytical tasks. The percentages shift for managers: Dale spends about 40 percent of his time in analytical/quantitative tasks and the remaining 60 percent performing a variety of management responsibilities including looking at what other states are doing in their lotteries, checking out the lottery industry, directing the analysts, participating in meetings to anticipate research marketing needs, and making long-range plans. Dale explains that "Marketing research has to have the data to support a position, to influence decisions. The key is not getting so close to your opinions or so tied to a particular conclusion that you can't accept other people's views."

Insurance Sales

Insurance agents and brokers help individuals or companies select the right policy for their needs for financial protection against loss. Licensed agents are qualified to advise about insurance protection for automobiles, homes, businesses, or other properties. They also can help clients maintain records and settle claims.

Insurance agents may work for one company or be an independent agent selling for several companies. Brokers do not sell for a particular company but place insurance policies for their clients with the company that offers the best rate and coverage. Generally, insurance policies fall into one of these broad categories:

- life insurance that pays survivors when the policyholder dies (life insurance agents are sometimes called life underwriters); or
- casualty insurance that protects individuals and businesses from financial loss as a result of auto accidents, fire, theft, or other losses.

Initial Training

Many insurance companies prefer college graduates, particularly those who have majored in business or economics. A few companies may hire high school graduates with sales ability or with a successful track record in some other type of work. Although most colleges offer insurance courses, a few offer a bachelor's degree in insurance. Other courses that are helpful include finance, mathematics, accounting, economics, business law, government, and business administration. Courses in psychology, sociology, education, and public speaking also can be very useful. The ability to use computer applications is very important, since nearly all agents keep their clients' records, as well as information about the various financial products they offer, on a computer.

All insurance agents must be licensed in the states where they plan to sell insurance. In most states, licenses are issued to individuals who have completed specified courses and passed a written exam. New agents usually receive training at the agency where they work and also, frequently, at the company's home office. Even after they're licensed, many insurance agents regularly take seminars and workshops to learn more about financial products and to improve their sales skills. In some states, such continuing education is required.

Earning Potential

The median annual income of salaried insurance sales workers is $25,000 according to the most recent *Occupational Outlook Handbook.* The lowest 10 percent earn $13,900 or less, while the top 10 percent earn more than $52,000. Generally companies pay agents a modest salary during a training period, which usually lasts about six months. Providing they meet the company's established sales goals, they are subsidized for about thirty months. After that, most agents are usually paid on a commission basis. The amount of the commission depends on the type and amount of insurance sold, and whether the transaction is a new policy or a renewal. Earnings usually increase rapidly with experience. According to a recent survey conducted by the Life Insurance Marketing Research Association, agents in their second year averaged $21,200, agents in their third year averaged $24,700, and agents in their fourth year averaged $30,400. Agents with more experience averaged $50,300.

In the Workplace as an Insurance Agent

Brent C. Sterns is a sales agent and manager of an agency for Shelter Insurance. His agency deals with both property and casualty insurance: homeowner's, auto, life, and business/commercial insurance. During a typical year, he writes 225 to 260 policies, of which 75 percent are for individuals and families.

BACKGROUND. Brent entered the insurance business with a bachelor's degree in Asian studies and a master's degree in college student personnel administration. This academic preparation isn't directly applicable to the insurance industry, but it has given Brent flexibility and provided him with administrative skills. Once he started working for Shelter Insurance, he went through two weeks of in-house training in Missouri, which provided him with an orientation about various insurance products such as homeowner's insurance or auto insurance. In addition, Brent attends monthly field training sessions with a district manager. These sessions, offered to all area agents, focus on marketing and sales information, covering topics such as how to develop a target market or how to prospect.

RESPONSIBILITIES. Brent's primary responsibilities include sales and marketing, day-to-day management of the agency, and some work with customer claims. Sales and marketing work primarily involves acquiring new business, which he does by prospecting, telephoning, and arranging for advertising.

TECHNOLOGY. Brent says that his computer system is essential. For example, when he's working with a client who is considering a homeowner's policy, Brent can feed essential information into the computer—information such as the cost of the home, its assessed value, its age, the fire code, the type of policy, and special endorsements for sewer and water backup or for computer replacement. Once all the relevant information is entered, the computer program will identify the premium because the rating tables are all computerized.

Addresses for Further Information

Information about careers in retailing:

National Retail Merchants Association
100 West 31st Street
New York, NY 10001

Information about careers in sales and marketing management:

American Marketing Association
250 South Wacker Drive
Chicago, IL 60606

Sales and Marketing Executives, International
458 Statler Office Tower
Cleveland, OH 44115

Information about a career as a life insurance agent or broker:

American Society of Chartered Life Underwriters (CLU) and
Chartered Financial Consultants (ChFC)
270 Bryn Mawr Avenue
Bryn Mawr, PA 19010

National Association of Life Underwriters
1922 F Street, NW
Washington, DC 20006

Information about a career as a health insurance agent or broker:

National Association of Health Underwriters
Education Department
1025 Connecticut Avenue, NW
Washington, DC 20036

Information about insurance sales careers in independent agencies and brokerages:

Independent Insurance Agents of America
100 Church Street
19th Floor
New York, NY 10007

National Association of Professional Insurance Agents
400 North Washington Street
Alexandria, VA 22314

CHAPTER SEVEN

Applying Quantitative Thinking

Careers in computer science and engineering require professionals with a hybrid background—expertise in quantitative theories of mathematics and science, and knowledge of practical applications in the workplace. People who have successful careers in computer science and engineering typically agree with most of the following statements:

- I have a good understanding of technical subjects such as math and sciences.
- I like solving complex problems that require investigation as well as personal judgment.
- I am comfortable working with computers and see them as useful tools for problem solving.
- I like learning new information on my own.
- I like applying theories to workplace situations to learn the how's and why's of applications and practices.
- I like fiddling with things that are broken or inefficient—computer programs, amplifiers, vacuum systems, old cars, light boards—to fix them, to figure out why they don't work, and sometimes to make them work better.
- I enjoy reading and talking about technical topics.

- I am able to work on several different projects at the same time.
- I can work well with various kinds of people.

If you, too, agree with these statements, a career in computer science or engineering might be right for you.

Computer Professionals

The computer industry offers a wide range of career possibilities that include programming, systems analysis, technical support database management, marketing and sales, electronic data processing (EDP), and information design as well as installation and repair.

Computer science is a growing career area. The U.S. Bureau of Labor Statistics predicts that most computer jobs will show a significant increase during the 1990s, with increases between approximately 40 to 60 percent in the number of professionals in some computer-related careers. For example, the growth is due in part to the move toward digital telephone networks, which means more software will be needed to run the systems. Another factor is the proliferation of less expensive and more versatile computers, which means that more systems analysts will be needed to integrate various components into coherent systems. More computers means, of course, that more data processing equipment repairers will be needed.

Initial Training

Professionals in computer science generally need a 2- or 4-year college degree, and for some complex jobs a graduate degree is preferred. They need to be familiar with programming languages and computer systems. Equally important, they need to be able to think logically, like working with both people and ideas, and be able to manage a number of tasks simultaneously. They need to pay close attention to detail, be able to work both independently and on teams, and have strong communication skills, both in speaking and writing.

Earning Potential

The most recent edition of the *Occupational Outlook Handbook* reports that the median income for computer programmers is $30,600. The lowest 10 percent earn $16,700 or less; the middle 50 percent earn between $22,100 and $39,900 a year; the top 10 percent earn more than $49,500. The salaries for computer engineers vary according to experience, but typically entry-level positions average slightly under $30,000; mid-level engineers with no supervisory responsibilities average slightly over $45,000; senior engineers in managerial positions average approximately $88,000.

In the Workplace as a Staff Engineer in Computer Software

Robert Carosso is currently a staff engineer with Bull Worldwide Information Systems, a French company with American offices and manufacturing facilities. Bob started as an associate programmer and then was promoted to associate engineer, engineer, senior engineer, principal engineer, and consulting engineer.

BACKGROUND. Before his current position, Bob worked as a consulting engineer in Bull's Unix Workstations Product Line Management; he provided engineering support for in-house and external development sites, training workshops, and trade shows. In his role as a principal engineer, Bob was project leader for office systems development. He was responsible for a range of duties such as design, implementation, testing, and documentation for software that performed a number of tasks such as previewing documents before printing and printing complex documents. As part of this job, he was also team liaison to a number of groups: publications, marketing, vendors, systems engineering, and customers.

Over the years at Bull (formerly Honeywell Information Systems, which was bought by Bull), Bob has worked on a number of software projects. Five of the major ones include an MS/Windows-based compound document preview program; buffered printer adapted support; image editor, print, and image workstation facility; rewrite of background hyphenation, pagination, and global replace programs; and rewrite of a word processing print program. As a result of his work on these last two projects, he was awarded two software patents.

Bob says that most of his high school and college education was valuable not for its content, but because that's where he learned how to learn. Little of the specific subject matter from his college education—even though it was in math and computer science—is directly applicable to what he does now, even though there has been an occasional specific course, such as systems analysis, that is still valuable.

RESPONSIBILITIES. As a staff engineer and project leader, he is responsible for a team of five other professionals on the data integration services team. Bob is the principal designer who makes the major technical decisions for his team, which is comprised of computer engineers who will write most of the actual software code. On this project, Bob and his team will work closely with the other two teams who are responsible for other aspects of the project. Bull's long-range goal is for these teams to develop frameworks for what are called "case computer tools"— that is, software that helps programmers do such things as create software specifications, write new software, and design new systems. The product these teams develop will be especially valuable because it will try to address problems with current computer tools, which are often built by separate vendors who make no effort to develop tools that communicate with each other. This current project will attempt to integrate tools so that an end user can use two or more tools together, something which is currently not possible.

CONTINUING EDUCATION. Bob has taken many additional courses and seminars on specialized subjects such as computer vision, computer graphics, and PCs and technical workstations. Ongoing education is a critical part of Bob's work. He says his most immediately useful information comes from what he studies as part of the on-the-job learning that comes with any new project or in intensive seminars. For example, in preparing for his team's new project, he has recently studied Unix C-language, the X-windowing system, and data base methodology. He has scheduled his entire project team to take a week-long course in C++ and object-oriented design, an advanced programming course that will focus on the syntax of the C++ language and then deal with the technique of object-oriented design that helps a programmer modularize a program with a "bottom up" design that is easier to reuse for related processes.

SUGGESTIONS. Bob says that school gives students a chance to learn a lot about a broad range of knowledge and the opportunity to gain specialized knowledge about a few things. But, he says, after the formal coursework, what really makes a person an engineer is the experience, the techniques of problem solving, and the ability to learn new information. He cautions, though, that there are a few other things that contribute to making an engineer as well, things he never expected when he landed his first job as an associate engineer. His communication skills are as important as his technical skills and his problem-solving abilities. Bob says active listening skills are essential, and interviewing skills are a must. He has to be a good technical writer, and, because he occasionally travels to France to work with his colleagues there, he's had to work at learning (actually re-learning) French.

When Bob started as an associate programmer, 75 percent of his time was taken up with technical work, the other 25 percent with communication. Now, though, 40 percent of his time involves highly technical work in designing computer software, while the other 60 percent involves critical communication—writing reports, responding to requests for proposals, making formal oral presentations, talking with customers as well as other engineers, and working productively with team members.

Computer Systems Analysts

Computer systems analysts plan and develop new computer systems or devise ways to apply existing systems to processes still completed manually or by some less efficient computer system. They may design whole new systems, including hardware and software, or they may add a single new software application to harness more of the computer's power.

Initial Training

Although systems analysts generally need a 2- or 4-year college degree, and for some complex jobs a graduate degree, both Deborah L. Duke and Janet Clemmensen show that there is no universally accepted way to prepare for this job. Many people enter this occupation from another one, such as computer programming or engineering, or as Janet did by starting in data processing and working her way up by taking courses and getting on-the-job training. In fact, most systems analysts not only have a college degree, but they also have relevant workplace experience—business management for a business organization and physical sciences or applied mathematics or engineering for a scientifically oriented organization. Systems analysts need to be familiar with programming languages and computer systems. Equally important, they need to be able to think logically, like working with both people and ideas, and be able to manage a number of tasks simultaneously. They need to pay close attention to detail, be able to work both independently and on teams, and have strong communication skills.

Earning Potential

The most recent edition of the *Occupational Outlook Handbook* reports that the median income for systems analysts is $35,800. The lowest 10 percent earn $19,900 or less; the middle 50 percent earn between $27,100 and $45,400 a year; the top 10 percent earn more than $51,600. Higher salaries are more likely in the Northeast, especially in mining and public utilities; salaries tend to be lowest for systems analysts in the Midwest, especially in finance, insurance, and real estate.

In the Workplace as a Computer Consultant

Deborah L. Duke is a computer consultant (actually a systems designer and analyst who works as a liaison between the system and the end users). Clients usually call her because they need some kind of data reporting capability from their current computer system or they need an entire system to be designed and installed.

Deborah specializes in using a fourth-generation computer language called FOCUS, which is more English-like than third-generation languages such as FORTRAN or COBOL. Using FOCUS, users can write a program that's more understandable; thus, clients can take over much of the maintenance of the system without needing to have a systems analyst readily available.

BACKGROUND. Deborah has a bachelor's degree in education with a concentration in math and science, and a master's degree in education with a concentration in research methodologies (both quantitative and qualitative analysis skills). She says her transformation from an end user of computers to an analyst was gradual. While she was in graduate school, Deborah worked as the assistant to the dean of the graduate school at Loyola University in Chicago. There she learned FOCUS since the dean's office was a test site for implementing FOCUS within the university. During those five years, she did a great deal to computerize the graduate school.

When Deborah left Loyola University, she worked for a year as a systems analyst for the Federal Reserve Bank of Chicago. As the only person on the team who knew FOCUS, she became the project leader. During the next year, she worked as a senior consultant and set up an information center in a California hospital. The system tracked the hospital's day-to-day processes—patients, personnel, pharmacy—and used the diagnosis-related groupings set up by medicare to generate reports. After Deborah returned to Chicago, she worked as a systems analyst for the next four years for a consulting firm. Then, a little more than three years ago, she set up her own independent consulting business.

RESPONSIBILITIES. When Deborah begins projects for new clients, she generally follows the same four steps. First, she hopes that her clients have actually identified the problem they want her to handle, but she's learned that this isn't always the case. So Deborah begins a series of interviews to find out what the clients want to do and how the business works. For example, a client specializing in health insurance might want to generate from one overall summary a series of reports showing specific details such as the ways patients spend their healthcare dollars, possible reasons patients go into a hospital, and the length of stays by diagnoses. Once Deborah knows this information, she can generally design what the data need to look like and how they should be stored. The time this step takes depends on Deborah's familiarity with the business and the complexity of task.

In the second step, Deborah develops a project plan based on what the clients have said they want. For example, if they provide outlines of the reports they need to have generated from the computerized data, Deborah can estimate such things as the specific activities required to complete each report, the time needed to complete each one, and the cost (billed hourly).

In the third step, Deborah actually starts the job. First, she needs to get the data files, which may be existing files; however, sometimes she needs help from other departments for access to files or to understand what a specific file looks like. Then she begins the bulk of the task: writing the program code and the very time-consuming task of testing the program. The fourth and final step involves supervising the program's implementation and training the company staff to use and maintain it. The duration of a project varies from a few days to a few weeks to several years, depending on the complexity of the problem and the nature of the data.

CHALLENGES. Two examples show how Deborah works on different problems. In one situation, a major insurance carrier wanted to learn more about the efficiency of their payment system including factors such as the way clients were treated, the accuracy of the information they were given, and whether they got their questions answered. Deborah helped this healthcare insurance company develop an attitude survey that could make connections between a specific insurance "product" and the healthcare services clients were receiving.

In another situation, a major food manufacturer wanted to know how well they were operating—that is, how well they were serving the customers (in this case, wholesalers). The overall task was to assess service, volume sales, and areas of marketing emphasis. The manufacturer had developed an internal measure to address this concern. Deborah helped them create an external measure to assess the customers' perceptions. One of the challenges was getting the manufacturer to use the same criteria for the internal and external assessments so that the results could be compared.

In the Workplace as a Senior Systems Analyst

Janet Clemmensen is a senior systems analyst for the Iowa Lottery.

BACKGROUND. Janet started working for the Iowa Department of Revenue twenty-three years ago as a data entry operator right after taking a three-month machine operations course after graduating from high school. Eventually she was promoted to data entry supervisor and then entered a programmer trainee program offered by the state and took evening courses in data processing. This background, along with extensive on-the-job training, enabled her to apply for a position at the Lottery, which was part of the Department of Revenue when it started in 1985.

RESPONSIBILITIES. Janet says that in a broad sense she is responsible for "designing new programs or systems and maintaining current programs and systems that deal with everything from employee and payroll files to data from the lottery games." The Iowa Lottery offers three types of games: an instant scratch-off game, a pull-tab game, and several daily on-line games, including Iowa Lotto with a Wild Card, Lotto America, and the $100,000 Cash Game. All of the information from these games—for example, sales throughout the state at various retailers—is entered into giant spreadsheets.

Janet often receives requests for information about various aspects of the lottery from internal departments. For example, recently the marketing department wanted to know which Iowa retailers had highest sales on one of the lottery games so that they could design an incentive program to encourage other retailers to invest more in games. Janet also designed a menu-driven program that lottery employees can access from their own computer terminals to check daily updates of data.

OBSERVATIONS. "Problem solving is a large part of the job," Janet explains. "You can't be discouraged if you don't get the expected results immediately. You have to enjoy debugging because a problem may not necessarily be how you've written the program. It may be the operating system." She downplays her quantitative background, saying that "number crunching is less important than having a logical thought process and understanding conceptually how a problem can be approached."

Engineers

Engineers—regardless of the type—apply the theories and principles of science and mathematics to solve practical technical problems. Their work is often a link between a scientific discovery and its application. Broadly speaking, engineers design machinery, products, systems, and processes for efficient and economical performance. In addition to having strong backgrounds in mathematics and science, many engineers need good computer skills because they often use computer-aided design systems to produce and analyze designs. They also need strong speaking and writing skills because they spend a great deal of time consulting with other professionals and writing several kinds of reports.

More than twenty-five major specialties of engineering are recognized by professional societies. Within these major branches are numerous subdivisions. For example, structural, environmental, and transportation engineering are subdivisions of civil engineering. Engineers also may specialize in one industry, such as motor vehicles or batteries, or in one field of technology such as propulsion or guidance systems. Ten specialties of engineering, including sources for further information, are discussed below.

Aerospace engineers design, develop, test, and help produce commercial and military aircraft, missiles, and spacecraft. They often specialize in areas such as structural design, guidance, navigation and control, instrumentation and communication, or production methods. Some aerospace engineers specialize in one type of product such as passenger planes, helicopters, or space-craft.

American Institute of Aeronautics and Astronautics, Inc.
AIAA Student Programs
The Aerospace Center
370 L'Enfant Promenade, SW
Washington, DC 20024

Chemical engineers work in many phases of the production of chemicals and chemical products. For example, they design equipment and plants, determine and test methods of manufacturing, and supervise production. Some chemical engineers specialize in particular operations such as oxidation or polymerization; others specialize in particular areas such as pollution control or production of a specific product.

American Institute of Chemical Engineers
345 East 47th Street
New York, NY 10017

American Chemical Society
Career Services
1155 16th Street, NW
Washington, DC 20036

Civil engineers work in the oldest branch of engineering. They design and supervise the construction of roads, airports, tunnels, bridges, water supply and sewage systems, and buildings. Major specialties in civil engineering include structural, water resources, environmental, construction, transportation, and geotechnical engineering.

American Institute of Civil Engineers
345 East 47th Street
New York, NY 10017

Electrical and electronics engineers design, develop, test, and supervise the manufacture of electrical and electronic equipment. The specialities of electrical and electronic engineers include major areas such as power distributing equipment, integrated circuits, computers, electrical equipment manufacturing, and communications. Subspecialties include areas such as industrial robot control systems and aviation electronics.

Institute of Electrical and Electronics Engineers
  United States Activities Board
  1828 L Street, NW
  Suite 102
  Washington, DC 20036

Industrial engineers determine the most effective ways for an organization to use the basic elements of production—people, machines, materials, information, and energy. They bridge the gap between management and operations. They are more concerned than other engineering specialties with the people and the methods rather than the processes and products.

Institute of Industrial Engineers, Inc.
  25 Technology Park/Atlanta
  Norcross, GA 30092

Mechanical engineers are concerned with the production, transmission, and use of mechanical power and heat. They design and develop power-producing machines such as internal combustion engines, steam and gas turbines, and jet and rocket engines. They also design and develop power-using machines such as refrigeration and air-conditioning equipment, robots, machine tools, materials handling systems, and industrial production equipment.

The American Society of Mechanical Engineers
  345 East 47th Street
  New York, NY 10017

Metallurgical, ceramic, and materials engineers develop new types of metals and other materials that meet special requirements. For example, these materials may be heat resistant, strong, and lightweight. Most metallurgical engineers work in one of three branches of metallurgy: (1) extractive or chemical (2) physical, or (3) mechanical or process. Ceramic engineers develop new ceramic materials and methods for making ceramic material into useful products. Ceramics include all nonmetallic, inorganic materials that require high-temperature processing. Materials engineers evaluate technical and economic factors to determine which of many metals, plastics, ceramics, or other materials is the best for a particular application.

The Minerals, Metals, & Materials Society
420 Commonwealth Drive
Warrendale, PA 15086

ASM International
Metals Park, OH 44073

Mining engineers find, extract, and prepare minerals for manufacturing industries to use. They design open-pit and underground mines, supervise the construction of mine shafts and tunnels in underground operations, and devise methods for transporting minerals to processing plants. Many mining engineers are working to solve problems related to land reclamation and water and air pollution.

The Society of Mining Engineers, Inc.
P.O. Box 625002
Littleton, CO 80127-5002

Nuclear engineers design, develop, monitor, and operate nuclear power plants used to generate electricity and power Navy ships. They also conduct research on nuclear energy and radiation. They may work on the nuclear fuel cycle, on breeder reactors, or fusion energy. Many work to develop industrial and medical uses for radioactive materials.

American Nuclear Society
   555 North Kensington Avenue
   LaGrange Park, IL 60525

Petroleum engineers explore and drill for gas and oil. Many plan and supervise drilling operations. Since only a small proportion of the gas or oil in a reservoir will flow out under natural forces, petroleum engineers develop and use various enhanced recovery methods.

Society of Petroleum Engineers
   P.O. Box 833836
   Richardson, TX 75083-3836

According to the most recent figures from the U.S. Bureau of Labor Statistics, the job outlook for most engineering specialties is average to very good. Engineering professions that are expected to grow between now and the year 2000 include aerospace; chemical; civil; electrical and electronic; industrial; mechanical; and metallurgical, ceramic, and materials. Engineering professions that are expected to remain stable or decline slightly between now and the year 2000 include mining, nuclear, and petroleum.

Initial Training

A bachelor's degree in engineering is usually required for beginning engineering jobs. Occasionally a college graduate with a degree in science or mathematics may qualify, but such degrees usually are missing the necessary applied component that engineering programs include. Many engineering degrees are granted in a specialty such as electrical, civil, or mechanical engineering; however, engineers trained in one field may work in another.

While most engineers graduate from four-year programs, some graduate from five-year and six-year programs. Some of these extended programs offer students a cooperative plan that combines academic study with workplace experience (which also helps with the extraordinary expense of a college education). Another kind of extended program offers students the opportunity of earning two degrees: one version enables students to earn two bachelor's degrees, one in liberal arts and one in engineering; another version enables students to earn both a bachelor's and a master's degree in engineering.

Advanced degrees are required for faculty positions on an engineering faculty; however, many engineers earn a master's degree or a Ph.D. because they want to learn new technology, expand their career options, or have a stronger theoretical basis for workplace research.

Earning Potential

Starting salaries for engineers with the bachelor's degree are significantly higher than starting salaries for graduates in other fields. Graduates with a bachelor's degree average about $29,200 a year. Those with a master's degree and no experience typically start at $34,600, and those with a Ph.D. at $46,600. Starting offers for those with a bachelor's degree vary by field:

Petroleum engineers	$32,016
Chemical engineers	30,996
Electrical and electronics engineers	29,736
Metallurgical, ceramic, and materials engineers	29,448
Mechanical engineers	29,388
Nuclear engineers	28,740
Industrial engineers	28,476
Mining engineers	28,440
Aerospace engineers	28,176
Civil engineers	25,596

In the Workplace as an Engineer

Gary Tarcy is a scientific associate for the Aluminum Company of America. Fifteen years ago he started at Alcoa as a scientist. Over the years, he has been promoted first to senior scientist, then staff scientist, and most recently to his present position as scientific associate. He looks forward to additional promotions to senior scientific associate, fellow, and senior fellow (which is the technical track's equivalent of vice-president).

BACKGROUND. Before Gary came to Alcoa, he had earned a B.S. in chemistry and an M.S. in electrochemistry. He believes that the most important aspect of taking math and science courses is that a student "learns how to mathematically sort out and differentiate facts from artifacts," in other words to tell the difference between what's significant and what's trivial—and then be able to quantify that difference. He says he still uses what he learned in courses such as thermodynamics and kinetics, but that the undeniably best part of his college work was the research experience—"learning how to do research by actually doing it and finding out all the things that can go wrong."

Immediately after college, Gary received some practical experience as a lab technician. About his work at Harshaw Chemical Company where he was a quality control analyst, he said, "I learned lots of chemistry; it was a valuable year." He also worked as a technician on a pickle research project. He strongly advises anyone going into engineering to "gain some practical industrial experience."

Gary still takes courses, participates in training sessions, and attends seminars. Although he's attended seminars in areas such as time management and positive negotiations, he says the most valuable study he's done has been in three areas: more chemical engineering courses in electrochemistry, lots of statistics courses, and long-term work in technical writing.

RESPONSIBILITIES. Gary's primary responsibility is to provide technical leadership for Alcoa in the field of electrochemistry.

In particular, he concentrates on the electrochemical aspects of the aluminum production process and batteries. One of his recent projects has involved analyzing and designing optimum batteries for powering 100,000-pound industrial robots. He also has worked on developing aluminum alloys for electric vehicles and torpedoes and on developing methods of measuring current efficiencies and alumina control methods/procedures for the Hall cell.

CHALLENGES. One of Gary's favorite recent research projects involved working on a five-person team that was investigating inert anodes for aluminum smelting. The process of producing aluminum normally uses a lot of carbon (a normal cell goes through approximately seventy-five feet of carbon in one year), which in turn produces a lot of CO_2. The U.S. Department of Energy wanted to learn whether it was possible and practical to replace CO_2-producing anodes with inert oxygen-evolving anodes.

Gary said the project was fairly successful. Their team was able to design inert anodes that reduced the material by eliminating the seventy-five feet of carbon and replacing it with a three-quarter-inch of ceramic metal matrix composite (cermet). So the project is possible; however, it's a long way from being commercially available because of an alumina control problem. Simply speaking, they need a better way to control the concentration of the "stuff" that makes aluminum. If the concentration is too high, the process is inefficient; if the concentration is too low, the cermet is destroyed. Unlike cermet, carbon has some natural process signals that control alumina; inert anodes don't have this natural voltage signal. So more work is needed before what the team discovered is possible becomes practical.

Gary says this project was interesting and enjoyable in a number of ways. He was able to use his background of coursework in thermodynamics, kinetics, corrosion, and material science. What was more fun, though, was working as part of a five-person team where everyone cooperated to solve the problem.

CHAPTER EIGHT

Calculating Probabilities and Risks

Many organizations need to know the odds of something happening—from the likelihood that someone will buy a winning lottery ticket to the chances of Coke loyalists switching to Pepsi, from the likelihood that an increase in insurance rates will cover AIDS claims to the chances that mandatory airbags will save lives. A career as an actuary, mathematician, operations research analyst, or statistician would give you the opportunity to apply highly theoretical concepts to problems—big and small—that are part of our everyday lives.

Actuary

Should men and women contribute equally to a company pension fund? Why do young drivers pay more for automobile insurance that older drivers? What should the premium increase be for a company's medical insurance? Answers to these and similar questions are provided by actuaries. Actuaries assemble and analyze statistics to calculate probabilities of things people insure themselves against: death; disability; sickness; injury; unemployment; retirement; and property loss from accident, fire, theft, and other hazards.

In general, actuaries specialize in either life and health insurance or in property and liability (casualty) insurance; some actuaries specialize in pension plans. Although a few actuaries work for the federal or a state government agency, most work for insurance companies located in major cities.

Initial Training

Actuaries begin with a bachelor's degree, often in mathematics or statistics. A few are lucky enough to have a degree in actuarial science. Actually, many companies will hire applicants from many majors—economics, business, engineering—as long as the applicant has a strong background in mathematics including calculus, probability, and statistics.

Actuaries have a series of ten exams they must pass; completing the entire series of exams usually takes from five to ten years. Many beginning actuaries pass their first exam or two while they're still in college; others begin the exam-taking process after they've been hired. Virtually all employers provide on-the-job time (and sometimes training) to help actuaries pass these exams, which are given twice a year. The Society of Actuaries gives exams for life and health insurance as well as pensions; the Casualty Actuarial Society gives exams for property and liability insurance; and the American Society of Pension Actuaries gives exams covering pensions. The first three exams by each society cover similar information, so students don't need to specialize until after they've passed these. An actuary who passes five exams earns the title of "associate"; those who pass all ten exams earn the title of "fellow."

Earning Potential

The most recent information published by the Society of Actuaries and the Casualty Actuarial Society reports the average salaries, noting that they vary depending on geographic location and experience. New college graduates entering the actuarial field without having passed any actuarial exams average about $23,000 to $27,000. Beginners who have completed the first exam receive between $25,000 and $29,000. Those who have passed the second exam average between $27,000 and $31,000. Actuaries who reach the associate level (having passed five exams) average between $36,000 and $50,000. New actuarial fellows (who have passed all ten exams) average between $48,000 and $60,000. Actuarial fellows with extensive experience—that is, top actuarial executives—receive salaries of $55,000 to more than $100,000 per year.

Would You Make a Good Actuary?

Two professional actuarial societies—the Society of Actuaries and the Casualty Actuarial Society—have a list of questions you can ask yourself to help you decide if you should consider a career as an actuary.

- Are your grades above average? Are you an excellent math student?
- Are you inquisitive? Do you like to solve complicated problems?
- Do you like writing? Do you like talking with people?
- Are you interested in a range of issues: historical, social, legislative, and political?
- Are you self-motivated? Do you get results?

If your answers are "yes," you might seriously consider becoming an actuary.

In the Workplace as a Senior Actuarial Analyst

Brian Beckman is a senior actuarial analyst for Country Mutual Insurance, a company that sells property and casualty insurance. He has passed five of his ten levels of casualty actuarial exams. Because part of his job description is making progress on his exams, the company gives him (and other actuaries who are still working on their exams) one hundred hours of office time for each of the two exam periods each year. Brian estimates that he spends at least two hundred additional hours studying for each exam. Even after Brian completes all ten of the casualty actuarial exams, he will be expected to keep studying. All actuaries are required to pursue continuing education after their exams are completed. For example, they might attend rate-making seminars or loss-reserving seminars.

BACKGROUND. Brian came to Country Mutual Insurance with a B.S. and a teaching certification in math, two years of teaching high school math, and a year at another insurance company. He says that his most important coursework focused on quantitative skills—work in calculus, linear algebra, symbolic logic, and computer programming. But he also says his writing and speaking skills are very important because he is routinely involved in committee work where he has to articulately express his views and write reports. He says that some actuaries are involved in public speaking situations when they're called to testify at rate hearings.

RESPONSIBILITIES. Because Brian has not yet passed all of his exams, he always works under the supervision of an actuary who has passed all of them. Even so, his responsibilities are varied. An important part of his job is writing computer software (most recently he has used FOCUS and APL). He works both on the company's mainframe as well as on a personal computer to develop programs that aid in the actuarial process. He also uses commercially available software to do number-crunching analyses on data bases to help him make recommendations about raising or lowering insurance rates and changing policy coverages. This information serves as his support when he helps implement upper management's financial decisions. For example, when a rate change is needed, the actuary department recommends the actual amounts, which is considered seriously by the company's rate change committee as they examine a range of factors that will determine the final decision. Brian also is involved with recommending rates for new products (that is, new kinds of insurance coverages offered to customers).

CHALLENGES. Brian emphasizes that an actuarial department in an insurance company constantly reviews rates. As he explains why rates cannot be based on initial claims, he identifies some of the complexities that go into rate setting. Imagine that one hundred claims are settled on a particular kind of policy, something that might take years to develop, report, and settle such as certain kinds of environmental or industrial damage. Suppose that 50 percent of the claim losses are acceptable, meaning that the amount of the settlement matches the amount that the actuaries estimated such a claim would be. However, also suppose that 25 percent of the settlements are higher and 25 percent of the settlements are lower than the amount that the actuaries estimated such a claim would be. Then imagine that some of the claims are not immediately reported (as is the case with, say, damage caused by some hazardous substances where it may take years for a problem to show up). These late-reported claims also must be considered. The job actuaries have is to consider all of these (and other) factors to "identify pattern of loss development"—which will eventually stabilize—and recommend rate changes that accurately fit the situation.

Mathematician

We have records of mathematicians in ancient times, contributing to work in commerce and trade as well as in alchemy and astronomy. Today, mathematicians are still engaged in a wide variety of activities, ranging from the creation of new theories and techniques to the translation of economic, scientific, and managerial problems into mathematical terms.

Actually, mathematicians do more than calculate risks and probabilities. Mathematical work generally falls into two broad categories: theoretical—what is often called "pure" mathematics—and applied mathematics. Theoretical mathematicians develop new principles as well as new relationships between existing principles of mathematics. Although they seek new knowledge without necessarily considering its practical uses, their discoveries have resulted in many scientific and engineering achievements. Applied mathematicians develop theories and techniques (such as mathematical modeling) to solve practical problems in business, government, engineering, and natural and physical sciences. For example, they may analyze the mathematical aspects of launching weather satellites, the impact of new drugs on AIDS, or the aerodynamic design of new cars. Because mathematics touches so many fields, much of the work in applied mathematics is done by people trained in mathematics but working in other fields such as engineering, medical research, computer programming, and operations research.

Initial Training

Although you'll need to start with a bachelor's degree, most mathematicians have advanced degrees, whether they are doing research or teaching in a university. Nearly all positions in pure mathematics require an advanced degree. Work in applied mathematics requires study in the field in which the mathematics will be used. For example, you can use mathematics in fields such as computer and information sciences, economics, statistics, physical and life sciences, behavioral sciences, and engineering as well as business and industrial management.

Earning Potential

Mathematicians entering the job market with a bachelor's degree average about $27,500; with a master's degree, $29,600; and with a Ph.D., $40,700. Starting salaries are generally higher in industry than in government or educational institutions. Experienced mathematicians average between $35,300 to $64,900 per year, depending on the kind of organization.

Operations Research Analyst

Operations research analysts are problem solvers who try to improve productivity and performance in large business organizations. They deal primarily with problems such as business strategy, facilities layout, resource allocation, inventory control, and personnel schedules. Their goal is to provide managers with information to evaluate alternatives and choose the best possible course of action.

Operations research analysts use equations and mathematical models—simplified representations of variables in a problem—to identify the components of a system and to help explain the relationships between these components. By changing the variables in the model, operations research analysts can determine what is likely to happen under various circumstances. These mathematical models are usually computerized, so knowing how to write computer programs is an important part of this job.

The specific work that operations research analysts do varies by industry. For example, an analyst in a manufacturing facility might deal with modifying production lines for new products, while an analyst employed by a hospital might monitor the use of pharmaceutical and laboratory services. The relationship of operations research analysts to other employees also varies with the organizational structure. In some companies, they work in a centralized office; in other companies, operations research analysts show up in several different departments.

Typically, operations research analysts begin by defining a problem and learning everything that they can about it. Then they identify the components of the problem, a task that involves skills ranging from interviewing personnel to conducting library research, from searching data bases to reviewing accounting records. Once they have a good sense of the problem and its components, they use analytical techniques to construct a model for the specific situation. For example, a model of molten metal casting might consider variables such as the flow rate of the molten metal, its temperature, the pressure of the flow, and the coating of the casting. After running several variations of a computer model, an analyst can make recommendations that can help managers make decisions.

Initial Training

Operations research analysts have strong quantitative backgrounds coupled with experience in computer programming. In addition, they need to have good oral and written skills and work well with a variety of people. Many operations research analysts have advanced degrees in operations research or management science, mathematics, statistics, business administration, computer science, or other quantitative disciplines.

Earning Potential

According to the most recent figures from the U.S. Bureau of Labor Statistics, the median annual earnings for operations research analysts are about $35,000. The bottom 10 percent earn less than $20,000; the middle 50 percent earn between $25,000 and $42,000; the top 10 percent earn more than $51,000 annually.

Statisticians

Statistics deals with the collection, analysis, and presentation of numerical data. Statisticians design studies and surveys and then carry out and interpret the numerical results of these studies and surveys in a broad range of disciplines such as biology, economics, engineering, medicine, physics, sociology, and psychology. They apply statistical techniques to:

* predict population growth or economic conditions,
* develop quality control tests for manufactured products,
* assess the nature of environmental problems,
* analyze legal and social problems, and
* help business managers and government officials make decisions and evaluate the results of new programs.

Statisticians often are able to obtain accurate information about a group of people, organisms, or events by surveying a small sample of the entire group. For example, to determine the viewing habits of everyone who watches television, statisticians survey a sample of a few thousand families rather than all the viewers. If this sample is chosen to represent the entire population and the data are carefully gathered and tabulated, the results from the sample can be generalized to the entire population.

Initial Training

Statisticians need a minimum of a bachelor's degree, usually in statistics or mathematics; however, a number of other majors— for example, operations research or psychology—offer a sufficient number of statistics courses to qualify graduates for beginning positions. The required subjects you need as a statistics major usually include mathematics through differential and integral calculus, statistical methods, mathematical modeling, and probability theory. Because computers are used for statistical applications, you will find a strong background in computer science very valuable; many students elect a double major in statistics and computer science. Another valuable option is combining statistics with biological or health science, especially for positions involving the preparation and testing of pharmaceutical products. If you're interested in market research, business analysis, and forecasting, you can combine statistics with courses in economics and business administration.

Earning Potential

The most recent edition of the *Occupational Outlook Handbook* reports widely differing salaries depending on where the statisticians work. In the federal government, the average starting salary for statisticians with a bachelor's degree and no experience is $15,700 to $19,500. Having a master's degree increases this starting salary to $23,800 to $28,900. The starting range for those with a Ph.D. is $28,900 to $34,600. The average annual salary for statisticians in the federal government is about $41,300. The National Science Foundation reports a median of $46,700 for statisticians with a Ph.D.; in business and industry, $55,000; in educational institutions, $45,000; in the federal government, $55,000.

Specializations for Statisticians

As a statistician, you have a number of specializations open to you. Consider these possibilities:

- Biomedical research—for example, working for a hospital, for the Centers for Disease Control (CDC) in epidemiology, or for an organ bank.
- Pharmaceutical research—for example, working for the Food & Drug Administration or for a private pharmaceutical company.
- Industrial process control/quality control—for example, working for a major auto maker, a food processing company, or a consumer products company.
- Survey research—for example, working for the Environmental Protection Agency on hazardous substances, for the U.S. Census Bureau, for the Bureau of Labor Statistics, or in marketing research.
- Sports statistics—for example, working for a major sports team.
- Demographics and population—for example, working for the United Nations.
- Computer science—for example, working for a software company.

Or, you can combine your skill in mathematics and statistics with another interest.

In the Workplace as a Clinical Research Statistician

Carol Leininger has just returned to the United States after three years in Switzerland.

BACKGROUND.   Before going to Switzerland, Carol worked for four years as a statistician and systems analyst at BBN Corporation where she was responsible for developing and testing statistical specifications and documentation for medical statistics in a data base system. After the program developers revised the software, Carol supervised the testing to check that the software system was functioning correctly. For four years before that, she worked as a statistician in the RTI Center for Survey Statistics, where she participated in the design and analysis of a variety of surveys.

Carol has a B.A. in psychology and M.P.H. (masters in public health) in biostatistics. Despite her quantitative background, she says that if she had it to do over, "I would have taken more math in high school because I didn't take all the math that was available." She remembers basic statistics in college as being tedious and not very interesting until she got to experimental design and multivariate analysis. She actually surprised herself by deciding to do her graduate work in statistics. Part of her graduate program was working as a research fellow in the Newborn Intensive Care Research Group at Columbia School of Public Health. There she focused on the work for her thesis and also had a firsthand look at the New York City public health system. Carol believes that the biggest advantage someone could have in becoming a statistician (even more important than being good in math) is being willing to work hard.

RESPONSIBILITIES.   As a clinical research statistician in the biostatistics group of Sandoz Pharma AG, a pharmaceutical company, Carol coordinated international data collection and specified interinstitute standards for CLINTRIAL, a data base/date-entry system that holds clinical trial data on patients. Carol explains that in this database system, "checks and balances are critical; they're regulatory safeguards for the pharmaceutical industry." Patient data have to be verified and controlled for high accuracy, yet remain accessible to researchers. Part of Carol's responsibilities involved working with immunology and endocrinology researchers, supervising outside consultants, reviewing documents, conducting training sessions, and writing international SOPs.

EXPECTATIONS. All of Carol's jobs have required that she be very good in math, statistics, and computer science. Statisticians don't have to know dozens of computer systems, but they need to be able to learn a new system quickly and independently. (In fact, being a fast, independent learner is an important characteristic for statisticians.) But these aren't the only skills Carol has needed. Statisticians need to be very organized and keep track of details. Equally important, they need to keep an open mind—not only being able to see more than one solution to a problem, but being critical of their own and other people's solutions. Carol also says that statisticians need strong skills in oral and written communication. Good oral communication skills let them talk with colleagues about potential problems; good written skills are essential for reporting the results of studies.

Carol acknowledges that being a statistician can be repetitive, precise work; however, she says, "once you know the methodology, you can apply it in different fields. You don't need to specialize. It's a versatile profession as long as you have the analytical background." Beyond the statistical challenges, the most interesting parts of her jobs have been designing software and training people.

In the Workplace as an Applied Statistician
Sarah Nusser is an applied statistician who is the professor-in-charge of the Survey Section of the Iowa State University Statistical Laboratory and also an assistant professor in the ISU Department of Statistics.

BACKGROUND. Sarah emphasizes, "If you're going to be an applied statistician, it's helpful to have a strong background in

another area so you have a *context* for your statistical work."
Sarah's own background is in biology; she has both a B.S. and an
M.S. in botany, which stimulated her interest in quantitative
ecology—specifically, community ecology. She explains, "One
of the ways you analyze plant communities is using quantitative
methods, especially multivariate statistical techniques." For example, the research for her master's degree involved investigating pine plantations in forestry, looking at the effect of various
forestry practices on the surrounding nonpine plant community,
the plants that compete with the pines for resources. Multivariate analyses were used to describe differences in plant communities subjected to different forestry practices. The extensive use of
statistics in this work sparked Sarah's interest in statistics.

After earning her B.S.—and before starting work on her
M.S.—Sarah worked for eighteen months as a technician for a
plant ecologist at the Smithsonian. The field work she did
involved nutrient cycling in wetlands. After receiving her M.S.,
she worked for two years as a statistical technician for a plant
pathologist at North Carolina State University. She helped
design experiments and analyze data for ongoing research on
diseases of tobacco. Then, after she received her Ph.D., she went
to work as a statistician for Procter & Gamble's Regulatory and
Clinical Division. She worked primarily as a consultant for
preclinical studies. The preclinical part of drug development
begins with an idea (for example, how a disease works or how
drug intervention might stop or mitigate a disease's effects). This
preclinical work includes testing of hypotheses about ways in
which chemical compounds affect the body, which gives evi-
dence for approval to run clinical trials testing the drug in
humans. After two years at Procter & Gamble, she accepted the
offer for her current position at Iowa State University.

RESPONSIBILITIES. As administrator for the Survey Section of
the Statistical Lab, Sarah has a range of responsibilities for
twenty-seven staff and twelve graduate students. The Statistical
Laboratory provides support and consulting services to people in

other departments on campus as well as to people in state and federal agencies. The Lab has four broad charges. First, its members do operational survey work, cooperating with researchers in other departments at the university or with state or federal agencies on contracts to design, conduct, and analyze surveys typically dealing with agricultural, health-related, and sociological issues. Second, the Lab receives long-term funding from the Soil Conservation Service (SCS), part of the U.S. Department of Agriculture (USDA), to maintain the National Resources Inventory (NRI). This is a survey conducted every five years to identify the proportion of land in the United States that has different characteristics or uses: urban, crop, wood, wetland, water, and so on. The statisticians at the Lab assist with the design of the survey as well as with the collection and analysis of the data. The third function of the lab deals with another long-term SCS project to maintain several data bases, the most important of which is the Soil Series Descriptions, the official USDA description list of thousands of soil types. The fourth function of the Lab involves work on research grants from various government agencies such as the Bureau of Labor Statistics and the Human Nutrition Information Service of the USDA.

RESEARCH.   Sarah's own research has three distinct strands. The first one involves survival analysis; Sarah studies statistical methods appropriate for data that are "censored." These types of data arise when it is not possible to observe exactly when an event occurs; for example, a physician may know only that the patient acquired a tumor sometime between examinations. In her second strand of research, Sarah studies estimation of distributions from data subject to measurement error, particularly in relation to nutrition research. Right now she is working on the distribution of "usual intakes" of nutrients in particular populations, which are used to estimate the proportion of the population with inadequate nutrient intakes. Sarah's third strand of research involves sampling. One recent project involved estimating weights for data with high nonresponse rates.

OBSERVATIONS.   Sarah notes a common misconception about statistics. "Some people mistakenly believe that statistics is math. It's not. To me, statistics is a method of quantitative thinking that acknowledges the variability in virtually everything. Statistics provides a way to think about a problem, a way to study a problem and answer questions about it. Math is a tool rather than the object of the discipline."

Suggestions for Further Reading

Picture Yourself Making a Terrific Choice! The Actuarial Profession. Published by the Society of Actuaries and the Casual Actuarial Society, 1991.

Actuaries at a Glance: Minorities in the Actuarial Profession. Published by the Society of Actuaries and the Casualty Actuarial Society, 1991.

Seeking Employment in the Mathematical Sciences. Published by the American Mathematical Society.

Addresses for Further Information

For facts about actuarial careers:

Society of Actuaries
   475 North Martingale Road, Suite 800
   Schaumburg, IL 60173-2226

American Society of Actuaries
   1720 I Street, NW, 7th Floor
   Washington, DC 20006

Career information about actuaries specializing in casualty insurance:

Casualty Actuarial Society
   One Penn Plaza
   250 West 34th Street
   New York, NY 10119

Career information about actuaries specializing in pensions:

American Society of Pension Actuaries
   2029 K Street, NW, 4th Floor
   Washington, DC 20006

Career information about consulting actuaries:

Conference on Actuaries in Public Practice
   475 North Martingale Road
   Schaumburg, IL 60173

Career information about statistics:

American Statistical Association
   1429 Duke Street
   Alexandria, VA 22314

Career information about mathematical statistics:

Institute of Mathematical Statistics
   3401 Investment Blvd., No. 7
   Haywood, CA 94545

Career information about mathematics in noncollegiate academic institutions:

National Council of Teachers of Mathematics
1906 Association Drive
Reston, VA 22091

Career information about mathematics:

American Mathematical Society
P.O. Box 6248
Providence, RI 02940

Mathematical Association of America
1629 18th Street, NW
Washington, DC 20036

Society for Industrial and Applied Mathematics
1400 Architects Building
117 S. 17th Street
Philadelphia, PA 19103

CHAPTER NINE

Investigating the Biological and Physical Universe

P ursuing the biological and physical world requires quantitative skills. This chapter focuses on careers in biological and physical sciences such as biochemistry, plant genetics, forestry, and meteorology.

Biological Scientists

Biological scientists study living organisms and their relationship to the environment. Most biologists are classified by the type of organism they study or by the specific activity they perform. Recent advances in our understanding of life processes at the molecular and cellular levels have blurred some traditional classifications, so science is becoming more interdisciplinary. Still, these general classifications are used:

- *Aquatic biologists* study plants and animals living in water. (Marine biologists study salt-water organisms, and limnologists study fresh-water organisms.)
- *Biochemists* study the chemical composition of living things, trying to understand the complex chemical combinations and

reactions involved in metabolism, reproduction, growth, and heredity.

- *Botanists* study plants and their environment. One critical specialization is plant genetics.
- *Microbiologists* investigate the growth and characteristics of microscopic organisms such as bacteria, viruses, and fungi.
- *Physiologists* study life functions of plants and animals, both in the whole organism and at the cellular or molecular level, under normal and abnormal circumstances.
- *Zoologists* study the origin, behavior, diseases, and life processes of animals.

Initial Training

A Ph.D. is required for college teaching, independent research, and advancement to administrative positions. A master's degree is sufficient for some jobs in applied research or for jobs in management, inspection, sales, and service. Some graduates with a bachelor's degree start as biological scientists in testing and inspection or get jobs related to biological science such as technical sales or service representatives. Others become biological technicians, medical laboratory technicians, or high school biology teachers. Many people with a bachelor's degree enter schools in medicine, dentistry, veterinary science, or other health professions.

Earning Potential

According to the most recent *Occupational Outlook Handbook,* beginning salary offers in private industry average $20,400 for individuals with a bachelor's degree. Salaries for individual starting with the federal government are somewhat less: biological scientists with a bachelor's degree could start at up to approximately $19,500. Those with a master's degree could start at up to approximately $23,900. Those with a Ph.D. could start at up to approximately $34,600.

In the Workplace as a Biochemist

Marit Nilsen-Hamilton describes herself as a biochemist-cell biologist-molecular biologist, which emphasizes the interdisciplinary nature of science; a useful view that, she says, should be encouraged.

BACKGROUND.   She decided she wanted to become a biochemist in the tenth grade because of her fascination with fetal development. She learned about DNA, Watson and Crick became her heroes, and she went on to major in biochemistry as an undergraduate (sidetracked only briefly at the end of an unhappy freshman year when she decided she'd rather be an art major). The more advanced her studies became, the more she liked biochemistry. She rapidly completed her M.S. and Ph.D., both in biochemistry.

Then she and her husband, Richard Hamilton, also a biochemist, each were offered post-doctoral research positions at the Salk Institute with Robert Holley, who shared the 1968 Nobel Prizes in physiology/medicine for sequencing transfer RNA. They had adjacent labs at San Diego's Salk Institute, establishing a line of collaborative research that resulted in nearly all of their publications being coauthored. They stayed at the Salk Institute for ten years, working as independent investigators for the last seven years.

Finding jobs in the same place for two Ph.D. researchers working in the same field is very difficult, but ten years ago, they accepted positions at Iowa State University—Marit as a professor in the Department of Biochemistry and Biophysics; Richard to do funded research in the Department of Zoology/Genetics.

RESPONSIBILITIES.   Marit sees her position as having two primary responsibilities: teaching and research. Marit explains that she really does two kinds of teaching. One kind, she says, "looks like teaching." She usually has one or two upper-level undergraduate or graduate courses. Although she has taught large lecture sections, she prefers small classes where there's lots of interaction with the students. Her second kind of teaching is one-on-one mentoring with the undergraduate, graduate students, and post-doctoral fellows who work in her lab. Students learn the art and craft of science as apprentices, working with senior scientists like Marit. Initially students receive guidance in formulating research problems, designing studies, collecting data, analyzing results, and writing their reports. Gradually they become more independent. Because their individual studies are part of a larger project, students learn that science is a cooperative effort; Marit says that "Advances are made by many people working on many parts of a problem." The interaction in a lab is important; members of the team discuss problems, pose questions, debate the answers, and then argue about the interpretation of results. Marit explains that "science is an interactive discipline; hypotheses are really what it's about, so students come to recognize that 'facts' are evolutionary."

Marit heads a research team that typically consists of somewhere between three and eight graduate students (most working on a Ph.D.), one or two post-doctoral fellows, two undergraduate students, and a technician. She is primarily interested in a series of proteins that cells make in response to growth factors. The actions of growth factors, which are necessary to the growth of any multi-cellular organism, are believed to be most evident in fetal growth and in wound healing. She's interested in how cells in a multi-cellular organism "cooperate." *Cooperation* involves "communal" building of a tissue by laying down and modifying the matrix of proteins that hold the cell together. It also involves *communication* of messages between one cell and another.

Marit explains that research to investigate problems such as these "can't help but be interdisciplinary." For example, knowledge of biochemistry helps them purify the proteins and analyze their sequence, their activity, and their and structure. Knowledge of molecular biology helps them clone the genes for the proteins. Knowledge of cell biology enables them to understand the cellular response to growth factors.

The most exciting recent work of Marit's team comes on two fronts: First, she has discovered the receptors for what she thinks is a new hormone, a message-carrying cell that is released by the placenta into both the fetus and mother. One of Marit's graduate students has identified receptors in the uterus and mammary gland of the mother. One of her next problems is to identify the message, which probably has to do with coordinating the growth of the mother with the fetus. Another of the graduate students on the research team discovered an inhibitor of proliferation (cell growth) that is released from the matrix around the cell. This is particularly relevant for ongoing research on tumors.

SUGGESTIONS. Marit urges students to "find out what they're most interested in. If they do what they're fundamentally interested in, it will take them through a lifetime." But she also urges a broad education, explaining that it's a "big advantage for being able to handle things you come across." For example, she says being able to write well is important for a scientist: "How well you write helps determine how readily you get funded." A broad education is also critical in working with people, whether in teaching or in managing a lab. Marit says, "Research scientists today need a background in human relations and management as well as in science."

In the Workplace as a Plant Breeder and Geneticist

Arnel Hallauer is a plant breeder and geneticist who has been involved in corn research for thirty-five years.

BACKGROUND. Arnel earned his M.S. in plant sciences with minors in botany and physiology and then his Ph.D. in plant breeding with minors in statistics and genetics. Except for a two-year stint in North Carolina, he has spent his career at Iowa State University where he is currently the C.F. Curtiss Distinguished Professor of Agriculture. He heads a cooperative research team with four other Ph.D. researchers, twenty-five graduate students, and two visiting international scientists (this year, one from Yugoslavia and another from Hungary).

GOAL. Their overall effort is to improve the traits of corn—traits such as yield, maturity, standability, resistance to pests, efficiency in use of nitrogen fertilizer, and drought tolerance. They use statistics to assess the continuous distribution (rather than the discrete distribution) of traits in a population of corn. They work with corn's "germ plasm," the genetic source material that determines the traits. Each trait is influenced by an unknown number of genetic factors (perhaps between two hundred and one thousand). Arnel explains that "each factor has only a small effect on the total expression of the trait." So plant breeders and geneticists work with many genes, each of which has a small effect on the plant. They use statistics to estimate normal density distribution of traits in corn they are adapting to a temperate environment.

Arnel explains that "recurrent selection" has been an effective method of germ plasm enhancement. Recurrent selection can result in a 6 to 7 percent improvement per cycle of selection. Greatly simplified, this is how recurrent selection works: A corn *population* with progeny is evaluated and then replicated—that is, the data are summarized to get a distribution of the progeny and then 20 percent of the progeny with the most desired traits is selected to inter-mate to form another population. Then the process is repeated for three years, the length of one cycle. Arnel points out that these relatively small gains turn into "very positive results" after ten or eleven cycles.

When they get a stable population with desirable traits, they work to create a pure, repeatable *line*. These lines result from self-pollinating the same population for five to seven years; a pure line that is repeatable year after year. Each year, Arnel's team is working with twenty-five different corn populations and with eight hundred to one thousand lines (in contrast to commercial companies that may work with 10,000 lines) in an effort to find key inbred lines. The "whole payoff" comes when they "find key inbred lines" that are then used to create a hybrid corn with especially desirable traits.

RESPONSIBILITIES.   Arnel says that his primary responsibilities are to conduct basic research and to train graduate students. Arnel identifies several distinct areas for this work. First, he empirically evaluates theory and the expression of quantitative traits in corn as they are influenced by genes and environment. Second, he analyzes and interprets the data he's collected relative to these traits. Some of the payoffs from this work have been tremendous increases in the bushels per acre that can be produced. For example, parent seed stock can produce, say, 30 to 50 bushels per acre, while a hybrid corn might produce 150 to 200 bushels per acre.

This research also works to create corn that is more effective in its uptake in nitrogen fertilizer (so fewer chemicals are used), that needs reduced tillage (so that more plant is left, thus resulting in reduced erosion), and that is resistant to the diseases that sometimes result from reduced tillage.

A third area that Arnel and his team are working on is expanding the germ plasm base that's available in this country. (Currently we are using only 2 percent of the corn plasm available in the world.) For example, for the past eight years he's been working with a type of twelve-to-fifteen-foot high tropical corn that normally flowers in September, which, of course, is far too late to be productive in the Midwest with its relatively short growing season. Arnel now has it flowering in August. Why is this important? This tropical corn is far stronger than most commercial corn in this country; it is more drought and pest resistant, and the yield seems to be good. Yet, to hybridize the tropical corn with other adapted corn might take thirty years.

OBSERVATIONS.   Arnel recommends that anyone interested in working in plant breeding and genetics needs to take some courses that might surprise them: chemistry and biochemistry, technical communication, and computer science. "If you really want to understand the field, work with someone in the particular area." Plant breeding is interesting and challenging, but it has "lots of uncomfortable aspects. You have to see if you can do it physically. It requires some physical dexterity and tolerance for discomfort You have to be patient in this business. You have to keep plugging away. It's very time consuming because of changes in soil and weather."

Foresters

Foresters and other conservation scientists manage, develop, and protect the country's natural resources:

- *Foresters* plan and supervise the growth, protection, and harvesting of trees. They map forest areas, estimate the amount of standing timber and future growth, and manage timber sales. Foresters also protect the trees from fires, harmful insects, and disease. Some foresters also protect wildlife and manage watersheds, develop and supervise campgrounds, and do research. Foresters in extension work provide information to forest owners and the public.
- *Range managers* (also called *range conservationists, range ecologists,* or *range scientists*) manage, improve, and protect rangelands to maximize their use without damaging the environment. Rangelands cover about one billion acres in the United States, mostly in the western states and Alaska. They contain many natural resources and serve as areas for scientific study of the environment
- *Soil conservationists* provide technical assistance to farmers, ranchers, and others concerned with the conservation of soil, water, and related natural resources. They design programs to get the most productive use from the land without damaging it.

Initial Training

A bachelor's degree in forestry is a minimum requirement. However, due to the keen job competition and the increasingly complex nature of the forester's work, many employers prefer graduates with not only a master's degree but with some experience as well. Research and teaching positions increasingly require a Ph.D.

Many colleges offer a bachelor's or higher degree in forestry and range management. Forestry majors take courses in liberal arts, computers, and communication as well as in technical forestry subjects. Specialized range management courses combine plant, animal, and soil sciences with the principles of ecology and resource management. Few degree programs in soil conservation are available. Most soil conservationists have degrees in agronomy or agriculture.

Earning Potential

According to the most recent *Occupational Outlook Handbook,* foresters, range managers, and soil conservationists with a bachelor's degree working for the federal government start at $15,700. Those with a master's degree start at $23,800. Those with a Ph.D. start at up to $34,600.

In the Workplace as an Independent Consulting Forester

Chris Burnett is an independent consulting forester in the Upper Peninsula of Michigan. With a B.S. in forest biology and a Ph.D. in ecology as well as years of practical experience, he is well qualified to help private land owners and state government agencies manage forest resources.

BACKGROUND.   All of Chris' previous jobs have had an environmental/ecological focus. When he completed his B.S., he spent five years as an environmental educator and environmental consultant for Habitat Institute for the Environment. His primary responsibilities there included conducting water quality surveys for municipal governments and supervising and training college-age interns in a variety of environmental action projects.

After completing his Ph. D., he accepted a position as a wild-life ecologist for the Illinois Natural History Survey where he worked for six years. He had a number of responsibilities there. One responsibility was to develop a geographic information system of the natural resources in Illinois. Another was to evaluate the biological resources of proposed coal mining areas and to predict the impact of coal mining on those resources. He also conducted original research in diverse areas of wildlife ecology; the idea was to come up with multiple innovative uses for private, nonindustrial woodland management. For example, he developed a project to demonstrate selecting and growing shiitake mushrooms and evaluating the suitability of different strains of mushrooms. Another demonstration project involved adapting preindustrial European woodland management techniques (silvicultural practices) to current land management problems such as erosion in the Midwest.

RESPONSIBILITIES.   The process of forest management has three broad stages: evaluating, planning, and administering. Initially, Chris evaluates the resources of the forest land that the owner or agency wants to know more about, which may range from forty acres to more than one thousand acres. The first step is surveying the land, which involves locating and marking property boundaries. Then Chris delineates "management units" according to their physical characteristics. These "stands" may vary from five acres to hundreds of acres. The next step is "cruising the timber"—that is, estimating the volume of wood products and determining the market price based on the volume and type of product as well as on the market demand. When Chris is conducting the survey and cruising the timber, he also identifies features of special interest and/or sensitive areas such as water bodies and wetlands or special wildlife habitats. The final part of the evaluation involves identifying the landowner's or manager's objectives, which might be primarily economic (for example, to get income to pay the land's taxes), primarily to help wildlife (for example, to improve game habitats), or to create recreational/aesthetic areas (for example, to create an accessible aesthetic area).

The second major part of Chris' work involves creating and recommending a management plan for the forest land. His silvicultural prescription, based on the state of the stand and on the owner's or agency's objectives, can range from doing nothing to precommercial harvesting (weeding and thinning because the trees are too small to harvest) to many different kinds of commercial harvesting (for example, selective harvesting, shelterwood harvesting, clearcutting) to planting or reforestation.

Finally, Chris is responsible for administering the management plan that he proposed. He writes a prospectus—a timber sale notice—to determine who might be be interested in harvesting the timber and accepts bids. He also is responsible for preparing the timber sale contract and related legal work and then supervising the implementation of the plan by whoever wins the bid. He is paid either on an hourly basis or on a percentage of the timber harvested.

PREPARATION.   Quantitative skills, especially in statistics, are a critical part of the work that Chris does. For example, in a timber cruise, Chris is taking a statistical sample of the population of trees and then making relatively confident inferences based on that sample. Preparation for doing this kind of work included a wide range of courses in statistics: biometrics, multivariate analysis, experimental design, and exploratory data analysis. A number of quantitative courses Chris took while working on his PhD. (for example, computer cartography and GIS—geographic information systems) as well as workshops and seminars he's taken since then (for example, remote sensing, timber cruising, forest soil interpretation, and more work in GIS) are helpful in his work as a consulting forester.

TECHNOLOGY.   Computers are also a big part of Chris's work. He explains that when he does a survey, he starts traversing—the process of walking and laying out a circuit—by finding a known point (called a "corner") of section or quarter section. Sometimes he's lucky enough to find a permanent marker; other times it's some kind of artifact like a fence. Then he picks a direction and a target, and, using his compass, walks to it. He has a hip-chain attached to his belt, which spools out cotton thread to mark how far he's gone. When he reaches his target, he records the distance he's walked and the bearing. Then he repeats the process around the entire boundary of the land until he gets back to the beginning. He inputs all this information into his computer, which gives him a printout of the plot and the square acreage as well as the degree of error in the calculations. The software he uses—some commercial, some he's written himself—corrects for a number of factors including the slope and the lack of closure of the land surveyed.

OBSERVATIONS.   Chris explains that his job has an economic bottom line, but he says that "walking the land and learning the landscape of the region makes it worthwhile . . . seeing what's out there."

Meteorologists

Meteorology is the study of the atmosphere. Meteorologists study the atmosphere's physical characteristics, motions, and processes, and the way the atmosphere affects the rest of the environment. The best-known application of this knowledge is in forecasting the weather. However, weather information and meteorological research also are applied in air-pollution control, agriculture, air and sea transportation, and the study of trends in the earth's climate such as global warming or ozone depletion.

Meteorologists fall into three broad categories, differentiated by the focus of their work:

- *Operational or synoptic meteorologists* forecast the weather. They study information on air pressure, temperature, humidity, and wind velocity, and apply physical and mathematical relationships to make short- and long-range forecasts. They get their information from weather satellites, weather radar, and from remote sensors and observers. They use sophisticated computer models of the world's atmosphere to help forecast the weather and interpret the results of these models.

- *Physical meteorologists* engage in research. They study the atmosphere's chemical and physical properties; transmission of light, sound, and radio waves; and the transfer of energy in the atmosphere. They also study factors affecting the formation of clouds, rain, snow, and other weather phenomena.

- *Climatologists* analyze past records of wind, rainfall, sunshine, and temperature in specific areas or regions. Their studies are used to plan heating and cooling systems, design buildings, and aid in effective land utilization.

Initial Training

A bachelor's degree with a major in meteorology is usually the minimum requirement for beginning jobs in weather forecasting. However, many employers prefer to hire those with advanced degrees, and advanced degrees are increasingly necessary for promotions. For college teaching and research, a Ph.D. in meteorology is required.

Jobs with the National Weather Service require a bachelor's degree (not necessarily in meteorology) with twenty hours in meteorology, including six hours in weather analysis and forecasting, six hours in dynamic meteorology, six hours in differential and integral calculus, and six hours in physics.

Earning Potential

According to the most recent *Occupational Outlook Handbook*, meteorologists with a bachelor's degree employed by the federal government start at up to approximately $19,500. Those with a master's degree start at up to approximately $23,900. Those with a Ph.D. start at up to $34,600.

In the Workplace as a Meteorologist

Pam Daale is chief meteorologist for WOI-TV where she has been working for six years. Don't mistake her for a weather reader; she has bachelor's degree in meteorology, a major that is every bit as rigorous as mathematics or physics. In fact, meteorology majors are required to take math and physics courses throughout their academic program.

Growing up on a farm gave Pam her love of weather and her respect for it. She says when she was growing up, she "loved to watch storms." Since WOI-TV is in the middle of one of the major agricultural regions of the country, the accuracy of the weather forecast can have important financial ramifications for area farmers.

BACKGROUND.   While working on her bachelor's degree in meteorology, Pam completed a three-semester internship at the television station where she was later hired as chief meteorologist. After she earned her degree five years ago, a position opened up and she accepted it.

RESPONSIBILITIES.   Pam's primary responsibilities involve making a forecast, making graphics for it, and then presenting it on the air twice a day. Making a forecast involves going over information from the National Weather Service such as a numerical model that shows the weather for forty-eight hours and a series of maps that show those forty-eight hours every twelve hours (for example, Sunday 7:00 A.M. and 7:00 P.M., Monday 7:00 A.M. and 7:00 P.M.). The maps indicate conditions such as highs, lows, relative humidities, and atmospheric levels. Once Pam has these data from the National Weather Service, she is able to analyze them to create her predictions, which on any given day might include identifying areas of precipitation, clouds, and temperatures. The time necessary to make predictions depends on the weather situation. For example, if there are no unusual weather situations, analyzing the data and making the forecast might only take twenty to forty minutes. If, however, the weather situation is complex, it might take as long as two hours.

Once Pam has made her forecast, she needs to make the graphics to illustrate and explain it for the television audience. She works on a computer that has software with base maps to which she can add each day's features: highs, lows, sunshine, clouds. Using this computer, she generates a series of graphics that show how the weather pattern has changed and what she forecasts for the next twenty-four hours. She lists these graphics, including shots from the station's own radar, in the order that she plans to use them during her broadcast

When Pam is on the air, the graphics that she generated are projected behind her. In order to know whether she's pointing at the correct area, she checks the monitors that are positioned on either side of her and the camera directly in front of her that shows what's being broadcast. She believes that viewers have confidence in her reports because she can give reasons and explanations for what's happening.

WORK ENVIRONMENT. The difficult part of the job isn't the meteorology; it's having to "give up a private life"—the result of being in a highly visible position as a television meteorologist. "That's the one thing about this job that I don't like." However, despite being a scientist working in a highly public environment, Pam says that the job is interesting and varied, because there's so much variety in the weather.

RECOMMENDATIONS. Pam urges anyone interested in meteorology to "know a lot of math and physics." She also urges interested students to try hard to get an internship in meteorology—whether at a television station, with the National Weather Service, or with a pollution control company—to see what it's like day to day. The field is rapidly changing. Even now, Pam attends seminars sponsored by the American Meteorological Society (AMS) and various equipment companies.

Addresses for Further Information

Information about careers as a biological scientist:

American Institute of Biological Sciences
    Office of Career Service
    730 11th Street, NW
    Washington, DC 20001-4584

Information about careers in biochemistry:

American Society for Biochemistry and Molecular Biology
    9650 Rockville Pike
    Bethesda, MD 20814

Information about the forestry professions:

Society of American Foresters
    5400 Grosvenor Lane
    Bethesda, MD 20814

American Forestry Association
    P.O. Box 2000
    Washington, DC 20013

Information about range management:

Society for Range Management
    1839 York Street
    Denver, CO 80206

Information about soil conservation:

Bureau of Land Management
    U.S. Department of the Interior
    Room 3619
    Washington, DC 20240

U.S. Forest Service
U.S. Department of Agriculture
P.O. Box 96090
Washington, DC 20090-6090

Soil Conservation Service
U.S. Department of Agriculture
Room 6155
P.O. Box 2890
Washington, DC 20013

Information about careers as a meteorologist:

American Meteorological Society
45 Beacon Street
Boston, MA 02108

CHAPTER TEN

Sharing Number-Crunching Know-How

Sharing what you know can be tremendously satisfying. The careers discussed in this chapter all have something to do with teaching in a variety of settings—elementary schools, secondary schools, community colleges, and universities. Other teaching opportunities are available in vocational schools and institutes, government-sponsored programs (usually for retraining), in-house programs sponsored by specific companies, and the military. During the 1990s you will see an increase in the need for teachers.

Elementary School/Middle School Teachers

People who choose to teach elementary school (kindergarten though grade 6) or middle school (grades 5–7 or 5–8, depending on the school system) are responsible for introducing the basic concepts of numeracy and providing opportunities for children to develop skill in using these concepts. Although some children enter school with basic numeracy concepts (counting to ten, knowing how many pennies equal one nickel, taking one-half of a cookie), many others don't even know this much. Elementary teachers get the opportunity not only to teach these concepts, but also to instill understanding of the ways in which numeracy is part of everyday life. In many elementary schools, teachers work as part of a team, with one teacher responsible for teaching quantitative skills to students.

Initial Training

Elementary teachers in public schools and certified private schools need to have a bachelor's degree, usually in elementary education, and complete an approved teacher education program. All states and the District of Columbia require that teachers be licensed and/or certified by taking a specific series of college courses as well as participating in student teaching. Usually teachers can be certified in early childhood education (usually nursery school through grade 3), elementary grades (usually grades 1 through 6 or 8), or in a special subject such as reading, music, bilingual education, speech, or special education.

Requirements for certification vary by state; however, they typically include at least a bachelor's degree from an accredited four-year program and the completion of an approved teacher education program, which includes student teaching. In some states, new teachers need to have completed a five-year program in which they earn a bachelor's degree and a master's degree. Preservice teachers take courses in the subject areas they're planning to teach (math, science, social studies, literature, composition, music, art) as well as in professional education courses (philosophy of education, psychology of learning, teaching methods). Many states have grade point average requirements.

Many states now also require teachers to pass national, state, and sometimes local teacher tests for competency in basic skills, teaching skills, and subject matter. And nearly all states require additional education (a master's degree) for renewal of a certification. Employment for elementary school teachers is expected to grow about as fast as the average for all occupations through the year 2000 as enrollments increase and class sizes decrease.

Potential Earnings

According to the National Educational Association, public elementary school teachers averaged about $28,900, as reported in the most recent issue of the *Occupational Outlook Handbook*. Generally, salaries are higher in the mid-Atlantic and far western states. Earnings in private school were generally lower. Most teachers belong to unions that bargain with the school system over wages, hours, and the terms and conditions of employment

In the Workplace as an Elementary Teacher

Shelva Boyd is a fifth-grade teacher who specializes in teaching math, computer skills, language arts, and social studies at Fellows School. (One of her colleagues teaches science and reading to the same students.) In 1991, she received a Presidential Award for Excellence in teaching elementary mathematics.

BACKGROUND.   Shelly earned a bachelor's degree with a double major in elementary education and secondary English. Her master's degree in education has a major in elementary administration. She is currently working on her Ph.D. in curriculum and instructional technology, concentrating her research on the relationship between gender and math/computer anxiety.

She has a total of thirty years of teaching elementary school grades 2–5 in the Midwest (Illinois, Indiana, Iowa, and Ohio) and one year in Germany. For twenty-four of those years, she has been teaching fifth grade. For six years, Shelly was a collaborator with the Teachers on Television (TOT) program, part of the College of Education. Segments of a continuous live television broadcast originating from her classroom were required viewing for preservice teachers. This program received an award from the Association of Teacher Educators as an "Outstanding Teacher Preparation Program." She also regularly teaches in an accelerated summer program—one course for gifted students, giving special attention to math for girls, and another in computer math, logic, and problem solving for grades 3–8.

Like most good teachers, Shelly has done more than teach fifth grade. Among other things, she's worked as a nanny, as a test technician in a metallurgical lab, and as a writer for the Beef Industry Council. She's also written a great deal of curriculum about subjects ranging from outdoor education to state history. Recently, she has added to her work load by teaching a course in elementary methods in mathematics for preservice teachers.

APPROACH. Shelly identifies academic subjects for her students as falling into two broad categories. The first category, *problem solving,* includes things such as math, computers, science, and research in social sciences. The second category, *communication,* includes things such as language arts, reading, and writing. Shelly believes in an integrated approach to teaching because information and skills don't exist in isolation. They should have a context, a real-world application so that students can see that almost any task requires both problem solving and communication, and that there are connections between what they learn in school and their lives outside of school. Shelly's integrated approach encourages her students to use multiple skills, so they learn to apply questioning skills, critical reading skills, and analytical strategies to any kind of problem—from figuring out the cost of supplies for a class party to identifying the possible bias of an article about hazardous waste.

In implementing the standards recommended by the National Council of Teachers of Mathematics (NCTM) to make math relevant, Shelly sees the computer as a powerful tool that gives students a way to integrate math with communication skills for specific purposes. For example, her students use their computer software to plan a pizza party. The integrated skills they use enable them to do such things as write invitations, determine their costs for decorations and food, and estimate the preparation time. They may gather problem-solving information by making telephone calls, visiting supermarkets, or investigating news-paper ads.

Students in her class usually work in pairs when they're solving problems on the computer because of the support they can give each other. As they work on a problem, they keep track of their individual questions in learning logs and then meet in small groups to pose as many possible answers to these questions as the group can come up with. Then the whole class meets to consolidate the answers and select the most likely responses. Shelly says the key is encouraging all responses, welcoming multiple solutions to problems so that students gradually gain confidence and comfort in using this process. The evaluation of the responses is provided by the students, not by the teacher, which is "really a change from the way most teachers work."

SUGGESTIONS.   Shelly reminds anyone who wants to teach that it is a demanding job that requires high energy, creativity, and patience. While 75 percent of the job is working with students, another 25 percent involves supervisory tasks such as completing administrative forms, making contacts, holding conferences with parents, writing reports and evaluations, and participating in administrative and staff development meetings.

Flexibility is the key because things seldom go as planned in the classroom. For instance, if there's a dramatic rainstorm while students are trying to learn long division, you might as well turn their attention to studying rain. Long division can wait a little while. Teachers need to have multiple strategies to meet the needs of students with different learning styles. Finally, teachers need to be committed to helping their students feel good about themselves and to developing strong self-images and confidence in their own abilities.

High School Teachers

Secondary school teachers (grades 7–12 in some schools, 9–12 in others) are responsible for helping students to learn and apply disciplinary knowledge. High school math teachers deal with a curriculum that usually includes algebra, geometry, trigonometry, and calculus. More recently, math teachers also have included courses such as practical living, which focus on everyday applications of quantitative skills such as filing tax forms and maintaining a checking account. Many schools also offer advanced placement courses in economics, accounting, bookkeeping, and computer science. A similar range of courses is available in other quantitative disciplines such as computer science.

Secondary school teachers in most states are required to have a bachelor's degree in a specific subject area in addition to certification from completing an approved teacher education program. Just like elementary teachers, in some states, new secondary teachers need to have completed a five-year program in which they earn a bachelor's degree and a master's degree. Many states now also require teachers to pass national, state, and sometimes local teacher tests for competency in basic skills, teaching skills, and subject matter.

Initial Training

All states and the District of Columbia require that secondary teachers be licensed and/or certified by taking a specific series of college courses as well as participating in student teaching. Certification is generally for one or several related subjects. Requirements for certification vary from state to state; however, all states require at least a bachelor's degree from an accredited four-year program, completion of an approved teacher education program with a prescribed number of subject and education credits, and supervised student teaching in a secondary school. Many states have grade point average requirements.

Most states offer alternative teacher certification programs for people who have college training in the subject they will teach but not the necessary education courses required for a regular certificate. Typically these people receive a provisional certification and then teach under the close supervision of an experienced educator; after one to two years, they receive regular certification. In other states, they must take the necessary education courses to meet certification requirements.

Many states now also require teachers to pass national, state, and sometimes local teacher tests for competency in basic skills, teaching skills, and subject matter. And nearly all states require additional education (a master's degree) for renewal of a certification. Employment for secondary teachers is expected to grow about as fast as the average for all occupations through the year 2000 as high school enrollments increase.

Potential Earnings

According to the National Educational Association, public secondary school teachers average about $30,300, as reported in the most recent issue of the *Occupational Outlook Handbook.* In some schools teachers receive extra pay for coaching sports and working with students in extracurricular activities. Generally, salaries are higher in the mid-Atlantic and far western states. Earnings in private schools are generally lower. Most teachers belong to unions that bargain with the school system over wages, hours, and the terms and conditions of employment.

In the Workplace as a High School Math Teacher

Tony Vander Zyl is a math teacher at Ames High School, which currently enrolls 1,300 students in grades 9–12. The school has a good record since nearly 90 percent of the students go on to some type of higher education: 69.5 percent go on to four-year colleges, 10.5 percent go on to community colleges or other two-year colleges, and 9 percent seek other formal education such as vocational training. The ten math teachers in the department offer a broad array of courses: from general and applied math courses to statistics to two levels of advanced placement calculus. Both of the Algebra I and II courses and geometry courses have two or three levels of difficulty students can choose from.

BACKGROUND. Like many other teachers, Tony has experience beyond high school teaching. He taught junior high math for seven years and then worked as a school counselor for seven years before joining the high school math department. For the past five years, he has taught every summer in a program for gifted junior high school students who complete a year of high school math during three weeks of summer school. For the past five years he also has taught evening division education classes in statistics and math methods for elementary teachers for a local university. Finally, with seventeen years as a reserve officer in the Army, Tony has taught a variety of courses for the Army's Command and General Staff College.

Tony has a bachelor's degree in mathematics, with a minor in physics and a certification in education. His master's degree is in guidance and counseling; his Ph.D. is in counselor education. Over the years, he's taken additional graduate courses in teaching both at the local university and through state educational agencies. His strong background in education leads him to suggest that people considering careers as high school math teachers take all the educational methodology courses they can. "Knowing the subject matter isn't enough; you have to know how to teach it." He also suggests that people obtain more than one teaching certification (say, mathematics and physics) and plan to go on for an advanced degree. And finally, "Make sure you love working with kids."

RESPONSIBILITIES. Tony spends about 70 percent of his time doing what he sees as his primary responsibility—teaching classes. (This year he's taught statistics and algebra.) He believes that "problem-solving and higher-level thinking skills need to be central to what is taught." He says that once the class is over, "the algorithms (the procedures) we teach are forgotten; the lasting thing is how to think." Memorizing tables and formulas is fine, but "it's stuff you can look up if you need to." In the years Tony has been teaching, he says the "real change in emphasis is in understanding concepts rather than memorizing procedures."

Students are now encouraged to ask why something works. "If you understand concepts, you can figure things out yourself." The remaining 30 percent of Tony's time is taken up by nonteaching responsibilities. He estimates that bookkeeping tasks—grading papers, calculating grades, and writing recommendations—eat up another 20 percent of his time. The remaining time is divided approximately equally between working with individual students in the department's Help Center, which is adjacent to faculty offices, and completing supervisory duties such as monitoring study halls.

TECHNOLOGY.   Technology also has caused a big change, but using the technology (calculators and computers) has to be balanced with understanding the concepts. Students now can use graphing calculators (which are really minicomputers) that graph and solve equations. For example, imagine students are solving a second-degree equation. They could find the two solutions first by factoring or by using a quadratic formula, and then they could graph the function on their graphing calculator, which helps them visualize the problem. The graphing calculator expands the range of problems that can be solved since factoring works in less than 1 percent of the equations the students will encounter.

RESEARCH.   In addition to his Ames High School responsibilities, Tony has presented sessions at the state math conference and written journal articles about both teaching and research. Two of his recent research projects have involved examining gender bias in accelerated math classes and assessing math anxiety in high school programs and reducing it with audiotaped treatment.

College and University Math Teachers

College and university faculty teach and advise over twelve million full-time and part-time college students and perform a significant part of the research that is conducted in our country.

Despite their commitment to advancing the knowledge in their discipline through research and publication, many faculty members see teaching students as their primary obligation.

Initial Training

Most full-time college and university professors are in one of four academic ranks: professor, associate professor, assistant professor, or instructor. Some two-year colleges and community colleges do not have ranks. Most full-time faculty at four-year schools have doctoral degrees. At two-year colleges and community colleges, some full-time faculty may have master's degrees. Temporary or part-time faculty in both two-year and four-year colleges may hold master's degrees or be doctoral candidates. A person with only a bachelor's degree is unlikely to teach in most colleges.

Doctoral programs usually take four to seven years of full-time study beyond a bachelor's degree. Candidates usually specialize in a subfield of a discipline, but also take courses covering the whole discipline. Their work includes a dissertation, which is a report on original research to answer some significant question in the field.

Advancement through academic ranks at four-year universities (schools with graduate programs and faculty members who conduct research) requires excellence in teaching, research, publication, and/or service to the institution. The weight given to each category differs according to the type of institution. Newly hired faculty serve a temporary or probationary period (usually seven years). If the review in each of the categories is favorable according to that institution's standards, the person is granted tenure (which means the person cannot be fired without just cause and due process). Similar standards are used for promotion to each rank. In some two-year colleges, community colleges, and undergraduate four-year colleges, promotion and tenure are based far more on teaching and service than on research and publication.

Potential Earnings

Income varies according to faculty rank, the type of institution, and the department or field. According to a recent survey by the American Association of University Professors, salaries for full-time faculty on nine-month contracts average $39,410. By rank, the average for full professors is $50,160; associate professors, $37,530; assistant professors, $31,160; and instructors, $23,660.

In the Workplace as a Community College Math Professor

Hollace L. Bristol is an associate professor of mathematics at Northwestern Connecticut Community College, which is one of twelve community/technical colleges in Connecticut. The thirty-two full-time faculty at this 2,000-student commuter campus are unionized; they spend twelve hours per week teaching and an equal time in class preparation, at least three hours per week meeting with students during office hours, and a minimum of nine hours per week in "service work" (for example, curriculum development, project committees, and departmental and college committees).

BACKGROUND. Holly has a bachelor's degree in sociology (along the way, she was an engineering major and a math major) and a master's degree in secondary education. She also spent a year at the Gestalt Institute learning about therapeutic practices and group process.

Holly started teaching at Northwestern Connecticut Community College thirteen years ago, part time for the first three years and then full time for the last ten years. Before that she worked in a Connecticut YMCA outreach program for disadvantaged youths for two years. She spent another year working with "trainable" adults in a private residential facility in California.

For the past year, she also has coordinated the Teaching Partners Project, a project working with twenty full-time faculty from the seventeen post-secondary vocational schools and community colleges throughout the state. A pair of teachers from the same school work together to observe each other's teaching, keep journals about their observations, and interview each other's students. The purpose is to increase awareness of their own strategies and teaching styles in an effort to improve them. Holly said the project was successful. Participants saw things they wanted to change, and it made a difference in their teaching.

In addition to her teaching at NCCC, she often acts as a consultant for elementary math teachers who want to know more about using manipulatives—hands-on devices to help gain a concrete sense of mathematical relationships and operations—and problem-solving techniques. She gives on-campus workshops and also visits area school systems to help math teachers implement the recent standards advocated by the National Council of Teachers of Mathematics. She says that college teachers need to pay attention to what's happening in K–12 math classes; the cross-fertilization not only will help deal with the isolation that some college teachers experience, but it also will enrich the teaching methodologies available to most college teachers.

APPROACH.   Holly says she "really likes the wide range of age and concerns of the students" because she is able to draw on their experiences during class. According to Holly's philosophy of teaching, one of the key things that makes a course a success for the students is their interaction. She sees one part of her job as nurturing class cohesiveness, which often happens in response to her openness and her willingness to acknowledge that students may have a high degree of math anxiety. She deals directly with these anxieties—she teaches relaxation exercises, has students keep a journal where they write about previous math experiences, and encourages awareness exercises to replace old, negative experiences with new, more positive ones.

Holly says it's "important to treat a class as a social organism," which doesn't happen if she just stands in front of the class and lectures. As a result, she encourages cooperative learning and "lots of small group problem solving" with different people throughout the semester. She must be doing something right; these techniques significantly reduce withdrawal rates.

One of the things that happens regularly in Holly's classes is that her students use manipulatives. For example, her students work with cuisenaire rods to see concrete examples of fractions and equations, and they use geoboards to gain a better understanding of fraction problems as well as area and perimeter problems.

TECHNOLOGY. Holly thinks that calculators and computers are a big help to students taking math in a number of ways. Students who need some extra help can go to the school's developmental studies lab to work with skill-building software. She signs out graphing calculators to all the students in her precalculus class. Although they learn to do the basic operations by hand, once they understand the concepts, using the graphing calculators illustrates the functions accurately and efficiently so that they can do more advanced work more quickly. She teaches a pre-engineering course in planning and drafting (CAD—computer-assisted design) in a computer lab. Finally, she observes that students with certain kinds of learning disabilities that make writing numbers difficult (and thus perceived as being remedial in math) may, in fact, understand the concepts and be able to do math when able to "write" with a calculator.

SERVICE. Sometimes as much as 50 percent of Holly's time is taken up with responsibilities outside her teaching. She says it would actually be easier to stay in her classroom and be involved as little as possible in the politics of the school; however, she believes it's important for her voice—as a woman faculty member—to be represented in administrative decisions about operations and policies.

RESEARCH. Her own interests focus specifically around the methodology of teaching mathematics. During her recent sabbatical, she investigated the use of manipulatives in concept formation. She's also interested in leadership styles and approaches to team building as well as the role of cooperative learning in outdoor education.

She's currently working on a college math textbook that incorporates her views about cooperative learning, writing, and manipulatives in teaching college math. This book not only acknowledges that some people haven't had much success with math, but it also includes a lot of approaches students can use to help themselves move from the concrete to the abstract.

In the Workplace as a University Math Professor

Elgin Johnston is a mathematician, a full professor at Iowa State University, who is as concerned with his teaching as he is with his research. He has earned his B.S., M.S., and Ph.D. in mathematics. He attributes part of his interest in teaching to having taken a course about writing proofs as a graduate student at the University of Santa Clara with a person he said was "a very, very good teacher."

RESEARCH.   Elgin's research started with his interest in the approximation of functions, considering mainly how complicated functions can be approximated by simpler functions. This initial work evolved into his investigation of geometric function theory—that is, the study of various aspects of geometry and how they're changed or preserved under certain kinds of mappings. As a normal part of his research, he has written articles published in academic journals and supervised the research of master's and doctoral students.

But Elgin is represented in this book not because of his professionally recognized research, but because of his teaching, on which he estimates he spends about 60 percent of his time. (His research takes about 25 percent of his time and program administration takes about 15 percent.)

APPROACH.   Elgin believes there's more to teaching math than having students do the problems at the back of the chapter. He teaches concept-oriented classes, bringing as many real-life problems into class as possible. He believes math teachers should try to vary their method of presentation from day to day. Some days he lectures. Some days he encourages discussion. On other days he uses a computer and an overhead projector and encourages students to make conjectures, to project possible outcomes. On still other days he presents a demonstration experiment so students can see if their projections work. Sometimes his class meets in a computer lab to work on modeling problems. And he's found that a "Jeopardy"-type game works as a fast-paced, interesti g review before exams. Do students like what he does? He says they're surprised at the amount of writing they have to do, but a typical end-of-course comment is, "I'm surprised at how this turned out, at how much I've learned."

RESPONSIBILITIES.   Elgin believes actually having good teaching at a major state university that identifies teaching as part of its mission is important. He says, "Teaching is what we promote, so we better do it— and do a good job with it." He also believes that good teachers can be strong role models for students. And when he comes right down to it, Elgin enjoys teaching.

About five years ago, in addition to teaching, Elgin agreed to take on the job as calculus coordinator for the department's sixty sections of calculus that are offered every semester. About the same time, the National Science Foundation (NSF) was funding "Calculus Reform" projects for five years. Because Elgin wanted to make changes in the way calculus was taught, he and a colleague applied for and received NSF funding to explore new, more effective ways of teaching calculus as well as ways to bring the computer into teaching calculus.

A large part of this work involves developing ways to incorporate writing into teaching math—not as a way to demonstrate knowledge but as a way to learn mathematical concepts. (Elgin notes that what they're learning in this calculus project provides information about "ways to bring writing into the mathematics at large.") As a result of this project, Elgin and his co-principal investigator on the calculus project are writing a textbook that "shows how calculus can be used as a tool to solve real-life problems and use good communication skills to evaluate and communicate." The calculus project also has prompted Elgin and a colleague to work on another project funded by the NSF to look at ways to use the computer in teaching mathematics.

COMMUNITY. Beyond his teaching, research, and service work at the university, Elgin is involved in doing math things in the community. He has been influential and supportive of efforts to develop a program for gifted students in the public schools. He is also the volunteer coach of the math club at the local high school. His interest in competitive high school math extends to his role as chair of a national committee that writes challenging questions for high school mathematics contests.

SUGGESTIONS. Elgin advises math majors, particularly those who plan to teach, to take courses in writing and to select an applications area as a minor (perhaps economics or physics), so that they have something else to bring to class. He suggests that people who plan to teach should take it upon themselves to make observational studies of their own teachers, especially the good ones, to collect effective models of teaching math.

Address for Further Information

Information about mathematics careers in noncollegiate academic institutions:

National Council of Teachers of Mathematics
  1906 Association Drive
  Reston, VA 22091

CHAPTER ELEVEN

Managing Quantitative Careers

M anagers are a critical part of every organization—from banks to credit units to wholesale distributors. With few exceptions, managers in an organization, whether the chief executive officer (CEO) or a department manager, have college degrees, often in the area that they are responsible for; in fact, many have advanced degrees. Some describe management jobs as having a high degree of stress, but the people in such positions often enjoy the pace and the challenges.

Chief Executive Officers, Presidents, and Vice-Presidents

Chief executive officers, presidents, and vice-presidents are the top decision makers of an organization who work with boards of directors to establish an organization's goals and policies. They are ultimately responsible for the failures as well as the successes of their organization. However, being a successful chief executive officer, president, or vice-president depends as much on experience as it does on academic training. Like other top executives (see chapter 3), these officials need expert-level knowledge, leadership skills, motivation, flexibility, self-confidence, and problem-solving and decision-making abilities.

Earning Potential

The most recent edition of the *Occupational Outlook Handbook* reports that the median income for top executives is approximately $38,700. Many earn considerably more than $52,000, depending on factors such as the level of responsibility and the type, size, and location of the firm. Top executives often receive additional compensation in the form of bonuses, stock awards, and cash-equivalent fringe benefits such as company-paid insurance premiums or the use of a company car. Chief executive officers (CEOs) are the most highly paid top-level managers. The *Occupational Outlook Handbook* reports that a survey of top corporations revealed that more than 150 CEOs receive base salaries of $1 million or more. However, a top-level manager in a very large corporation can earn ten times as much as a counterpart in a small organization and salaries are influenced by geographic location as well as the type of organization.

In the Workplace as a Chief Executive Officer

As president and chief executive officer (CEO) of the ISU Credit Union, David Slaughter manages a credit union for all university employees that annually invests about $60,000,000 for its members. Given the state of the national economy, David is pleased with the steady 8 to 10 percent that credit union members usually earn on their investments. Before accepting his current position, he had a number of jobs, including the director of accounting for a large public hospital in Texas. Before that he was vice-president of accounting and then president of a credit union in Dallas.

BACKGROUND.   David advises that people wanting to work in credit unions need a strong background in accounting and finance, but they also need a conceptual understanding of the complex processes that are involved. He says, "Without a numbers background, it's too easy to get blindsided. . . . While some things can't be quantified, this is ultimately a numbers business." David's own background includes a B.S. in accounting with a minor in finance. He emphasizes that there's continual on-the-job education. On his own, he has acquired expertise in public relations, personnel management, and politics. Part of David's early knowledge about credit unions came from working as a volunteer, a practice he encourages and recommends to others.

RESPONSIBILITIES.   As president and CEO, David is responsible for overseeing the policies and implementing the procedures established by the credit union's board of directors. He regularly advises the board of directors "about what's going on." However, because the board is composed entirely of volunteers, he also sees part of his responsibility as educating the members about the operation of the credit union as well as the factors that influence financial decision making. Finally, David is responsible for the supervision of the credit union's thirty-three full-time equivalent employees and the twelve students who each work twenty hours a week.

OUTLOOK.   Credit unions are consolidating: in 1980, there were approximately 22,000 nationwide; in 1990, there were approximately 12,000. Part of this consolidation is due to improvements in technology, which reduce the number of jobs. However, another factor is tremendous increases in expenses related to personnel and service costs. In fact, David says that the competition is "extremely tough." Part of the challenge in running a credit union comes from the deregulation of interest rates and interstate banking. But another challenge comes from the increasing role of nonfinancial institutions as major players in finance.

CHALLENGES.   Despite the entrenchment that is generally taking place in credit unions across the country, one of the parts of his job that David particularly enjoys is implementing ideas—for example, taking a client's idea and making a major improvement in services offered. Recently, in response to customer needs, he started a credit union mortgage department, which has developed to include home equity loans, home improvement loans, and mortgage refinancing.

In the Workplace as a Vice-President for an Environmental Consulting Company

James Gill is vice-president of finance for SECDonohue, a recent merger of Sirrine Environmental Consultants and Donohue & Associates. About 65 percent of the company's work is in environmental consulting, which involves recommending ways to fix problems such as disposing of hazardous waste. About 35 percent of the work is in infrastructure engineering, which involves design and construction oversight of airports, bridges, roads, wastewater treatment plants, and storm water sewer systems. SECDonohue has approximately 2,200 employees at fifty locations across the United States and has about $175-200 million in gross revenues a year.

BACKGROUND.   Jim has a B.S. in business administration with a major in accounting and has taken graduate courses in taxation. As a CPA in Ohio, he started work as an internal auditor for Champion International Corporation in Ohio, where he stayed for five years. Then he went to Texas to work for Oceaneering, Inc. Initially he worked as their manager of audit; then he went to Singapore for two years as their Southeast Asian controller. He returned to Texas, working for two years for Worley Engineering. After that he accepted the position as chief financial officer (CFO) for Sirrine Environmental Consultants (SEC), which was a division of CRS Sirrine. Eventually twenty-five employees (including Jim) bought out the Sirrine Environmental Consultants part of the company. They remained as an independent company for three years and then were sold to Waste Management, Inc.

RESPONSIBILITIES.   Until the merger, Jim was chief financial officer (CFO) for Sirrine Environmental Consultants. Now, as vice-president of finance for SECDonohue, Jim has taken on more of the finance duties while his counterpart from Donohue has assumed more of the day-to-day operations. Approximately 75 percent of the time, Jim is focusing on mergers and acquisitions; 40 to 50 percent of his time is spent traveling. The company has big plans for expansion—to be a $.5 billion company with 5,000 employees by 1996. Because of the general trend toward consolidation in environmental consulting businesses, Jim sees the growth of SECDonohue taking place primarily through mergers and acquisitions, perhaps twenty-five to thirty, over the next several years. Jim explains that big industries such as auto manufacturers with factories in different parts of the country are more likely to turn to one large environmental consulting firm that can handle the same problem as it appears in each factory, rather than hiring a different regional environmental consulting firm to handle each problem locally.

SECDonohue is currently seeking an international firm to become part of its organization. Although this international link will probably begin in the European community, Jim encourages the notion of "corporate citizenship," which "requires that we all help" improve the severe environmental problems in Eastern Europe, Asia, Africa, and Middle Eastern nations.

Jim's remaining time is approximately evenly divided among forecasting and budgeting, planning capital programs, and ensuring compliance with federal regulations. Every year, he supervises the development of a five-year strategic plan and the annual budget, which usually take two to three months (and two to three versions) to complete. Once a quarter, managers reassess the budget and advise the parent company and senior managers about the budget's accuracy and recommend any necessary corrective action. Once a year as part of the budget, Jim receives departments' plans for capital items (basically anything over $1,000 with a useful life of more than one year) and prepares a capital budget. Jim is also responsible for ensuring that SECDonohue is in compliance with all federal regulations since approximately 25 to 30 percent of the company's business is with federal departments and agencies such as the Department of Energy (disposing of nuclear waste), the Department of Defense (disposing of oil and various wastes on military bases), and NASA. Every time the company submits a cost proposal, the government conducts a pre-award audit to determine if estimated costs are reasonable; part of Jim's responsibility is to lead these auditors through the proposals. Then once a year, any awarded cost contracts will undergo an incurred-cost audit to make sure the government has not been overcharged; similarly, once a year Jim must file a disclosure statement to explain accounting and estimating procedures.

CHALLENGES.   One of the interesting problems Jim has to face is how to establish the value of a company that SECDonohue wants to purchase. What he wants to end up with is a "valuation ladder to determine what the range is for the value of the company," so he uses a variety of methods of valuation. He begins by gathering historical information about the "candidate" and preparing an estimate about their future profitability and reputation. Several valuation methods include (1) using the historical data to project future value, (2) finding sales of companies of a similar type and size (much like market comparison in residential real estate), or (3) multiplying book value of the company by some factor.

Managers

Managers work with the chief executive officers and other executives to make decisions that affect their department or branch or division in an organization. Like other decision makers (see chapter 3), managers need expert-level knowledge and leadership skills. They also need to have excellent organizational skills as well as problem-solving and decision-making abilities. (Note: Many people discussed in other chapters also have management functions in their jobs.)

Earning Potential

The most recent edition of the *Occupational Outlook Handbook* reports that the median income for managers is approximately $38,000. Many earned considerably more than $52,000, depending on factors such as the level of responsibility and the type, size, and location of the firm. Managers often receive additional compensation in the form of bonuses, stock awards, and cash-equivalent fringe benefits such as company-paid insurance premiums or the use of a company car.

In the Workplace as Director of Materials Management

Mike Ness is the director of materials management for Mary Greeley Medical Center, a 220-bed municipally owned facility with thirty-seven departments, ranging from emergency room and surgery to obstetrics and cardiac rehabilitation. Mike is responsible for thirteen employees in several different departments that form the materials management group: purchasing, inventory/stores (which includes distribution), and receiving/shipping. The overall goal of Materials Management is to ensure that every department in the medical center has the highest quality products and services when they need them, for the lowest possible cost. Mike says that like all purchasing groups, his is concerned with quality first.

BACKGROUND.   After graduating from college with a bachelor's degree in history, Mike started at the bottom of the purchasing department for a manufacturing company, Sundstrand, working his way up to senior buyer. After ten years with Sundstrand, he accepted a position as a supervisor/manager for Bourns, an electronics company, with six to eight people reporting to him. Six years later, he returned to Sauer-Sundstrand (the company gained a new name while Mike was away) as purchasing agent.

In two years, he accepted the position as director of materials management for Mary Greeley Medical Center.

TECHNOLOGY. Anyone considering a job like Mike's needs to have a strong math background and a great deal of computer knowledge as well as experience in all aspects of materials management. He explains that computers are the backbone of materials management. For example, materials management receives electronic orders from various departments in the hospital and then electronically charges the appropriate department's account, keeps an updated on-line inventory, and does ordering from vendors on the computer. While new employees need to be trained to use specific applications, a foundation in computer fundamentals and familiarity with multiple applications are crucial. Through the years, Mike himself has picked up seminars and graduate courses as he has needed new information about an array of topics ranging from sexual harassment in the workplace to specialized computer applications, from hazardous waste management to personnel supervision.

RESPONSIBILITIES. As director of materials management, Mike does no actual buying for the medical center, instead, his responsibilities are entirely managerial. He emphasizes the importance of strong decision-making and communication skills. He said he can't overestimate the value of being able to make carefully reasoned decisions or being able to write professionally. In fact, Mike devotes a full 25 percent of his time on the job to communication. This part of his job involves a range of activities: identifying and communicating department goals to employees, conducting meetings in his department, writing reports, and attending meetings with managers of other departments.

Another 20 percent of Mike's time is spent planning and organizing. He needs to make sure that his department has the personnel, financial support, and material resources to accomplish its goals. For example, in order to do their jobs, the employees in receiving need such things as forklift trucks, bar coders, computers, and staff training (for everything from fork-lifts to computers). He explains that part of planning and organizing is drafting documents that specify the policies and procedures that employees should follow in completing their jobs.

Mike also devotes 20 percent of his time to supervision and employee development. Because materials management in the medical center is new—only two years old—there is still a great deal to do in codifying policies and practices. He believes that informing employees about the materials management functions and providing in-house training will go a long way in helping them understand their individual responsibilities, reduce turn-over, and increase their effectiveness.

Budget preparation and its related activities take another 15 percent of Mike's time. He creates his own department's budget and also is involved in the purchase of all capital equipment for the entire medical center (approximately $6 million in capital equipment every year). Once the budgets are constructed, though, Mike needs to be alert to changes in operations that might result in changes in resources or personnel.

Mike gives another 15 percent of his time to establishing and measuring department goals and making sure that they support the overall goals of the medical center. A final 5 percent of his time involves ensuring the department's compliance with a range of standards and policies, ranging from following the municipal codes to adhering to federal commission guidelines (to ensure hospital accreditation).

OUTLOOK. In the four months that Mike has been director of materials management, he feels positive about what he sees as two major changes in his department. First, the entire department is now 100 percent computerized (as opposed to 40 percent when he arrived). This makes all aspects of departmental operation easier. Second, he has noticed a developing attitude of professionalism and cooperation among members of the department.

In the Workplace as a Sales Manager for a Wholesale Distributor

Robin Dye is a senior sales manager for Newark Electronics, a Division of Premier Industrial, which is a Fortune 500 company. Newark Electronics is an electronics distributor for 240 manufacturers. Newark Electronics primarily sells components; that is, semiconductors—the pieces that make electronic equipment such as computers, telephones, electronic doorbells, and various kinds of manufacturing equipment work. The company buys large volumes of components and resells them in smaller lots.

BACKGROUND. Robin started at Newark Electronics twelve years ago with a bachelor's degree in human nutrition and six months of experience as a hospital dietician. At the same time that Robin was deciding that being a dietician wasn't what she wanted to do, Newark was looking for new employees who were just out of college. Back then, her qualifications for the job included a college degree and a remarkable aptitude for mathematics. Robin describes herself as someone who has a good sense of numbers and what they can do, a "number friendly" person. As part of her undergraduate degree, she also had taken a good many business courses—statistics, accounting, business administration, small group behavior, and decision making. These skills, which have been honed by her years on the job, enable her to do the multiple responsibilities of her job, most of which involve number crunching. To do her job well, Robin doesn't need an engineering degree, but she does need to be able to read specification sheets and blueprints. And, like other Newark employees when they're first hired, she has worked through a self-paced electronics program to gain familiarity with concepts and vocabulary.

PROMOTIONS. Newark Electronics hires entry-level salespeople who have a minimum of a four-year college degree and two years of work experience. Promotion to senior sales is based on sales performance. Further promotion can move a person into outside sales management or branch office management, which is the route Robin has taken. Eventually, someone in outside sales or branch management could move up to a position as regional manager who, in turn, could be promoted to sector head (which is equivalent to vice-presidents of sales in other companies).

RESPONSIBILITIES. As a senior sales manager, Robin explains that a critical part of her job involves sales forecasting, making the projections about all financial aspects of her branch office, which may generate $2.5 to 3 million gross annual sales. To put this in perspective, the company as a whole—with two hundred sales offices in this country and a few in foreign countries—generates approximately $430 million in gross sales. This sales forecasting is such an important part of her job that 25 percent of her annual evaluation is based on the accuracy of her forecasting. Part of this work involves looking at raw data (for example, information about growth patterns, profitability levels, or number of employees) and projecting office revenues. In building her forecast, Robin considers a number of variables such as the branch budget for everything from operations to salaries to supplies. Robin says forecasting is a real learn-as-you-go part of her job; although there are some formulas, being good at forecasting is largely a function of experience and related factors such as general knowledge of the regional economy and awareness of customer plans.

In addition to forecasting, Robin is responsible for the strategies of pricing used by her office and for developing the contracts for specific customers. In order to do this, she has to know a number of variables, including the profitability of different lines, shipping expenses, and availability of the components. Robin also evaluates at least one hundred computer reports each month, reports that give all kinds of data on every account. Each report is designed to show different red flags (potential problems) in pricing, selling, or product mix. The enormity of this task becomes clearer when you realize that her branch office has as many as twelve hundred accounts.

Robin typically spends about 75 percent of her time in the office, usually about three and a half days a week. The rest of the time, she is on the road, visiting customers and making sales calls. She concentrates on difficult outside sales—lost customers who she wants to regain. She does the troubleshooting, and once she has the customer back, she usually turns the account over to a full-time salesperson. This kind of sales requires that she handle all sorts of complaints that these customers have, including problems with delivery dates, shipping, service, and quality control.

TECHNOLOGY.   In managing the multiple responsibilities of her job, Robin uses her computer a great deal. Her terminal is connected to the company's mainframe in their Chicago headquarters. When she wants to learn something about an account, she can check the computer; each account is listed in detail so information is easily accessible for her to answer questions and develop strategic plans. Because of the security risks, Newark Electronic employees are discouraged from using personal computers. In fact, to gain access to the Chicago mainframe through her modem, Robin has to use three levels of passwords that are changed regularly.

CHANGES.   Twelve years ago, Newark and their customers were "very male oriented." Now women in electronic component sales are less unusual, though Robin says about 80 percent of Newark's customers, most of whom are engineers, are male. Robin is encouraging to women and men who want to be involved in a similar profession and urges them to be firm about their interests and confident about their abilities. She said, "Take lots of math, science, and business courses." As a result of her own background and on-the-job experience, Robin is now involved in pilot test programs, developing new approaches that change how the company goes about doing things.

In the Workplace as an Administrator in Mathematical Science

Dean Isaacson wears three hats: head of the Department of Statistics at Iowa State University; head of the Statistics Unit of ISU's Agriculture Experiment Station; and director of the university's Statistical Laboratory. As administrator of this internationally recognized tripartite program in applied statistics, he manages a combined annual budget of approximately $3.1 million.

BACKGROUND.   After completing his Ph.D. in mathematics (which focused on stochastic integrals), Dean came to ISU to accept a joint appointment in mathematics and statistics. His research involves work in probability theory that has applications in a variety of disciplines such as engineering, genetics, and demography.

BALANCING TEACHING AND ADMINISTRATION.   Dean describes himself as a "probabalist who loves teaching." In fact, he says, "teaching is my great love." Even in his role as department head, Dean has chosen to continue teaching one course each semester and to retain his role as the coordinator of graduate studies, so he helps recruit thirty-five to forty new graduate students each year and then acts as their advisor for their first year. He also decides which graduate students each year will receive assistantships since the department only has assistantships for slightly more than half of their graduate students.

When asked to describe the changes in his career, Dean says that "Where you end up is not necessarily where you expect." Twenty years ago, he thought he'd be doing research and teaching for his entire career. Because of his ongoing commitment to graduate students, Dean admits that his own research program has slowed down. As an administrator he creates and manages the budget for the Department of Statistics, the Statistics Unit of Ag Experiment Station, and the Statistical Lab; builds teaching schedules for faculty and assists with the schedules of teaching assistants; determines committee appointments; and solicits funds from alumni.

RESPONSIBILITIES.   One of Dean's other responsibilities is serving on the Iowa Quality Coalition. This Coalition is a statewide effort by a number of groups including universities, private colleges, community colleges, organized labor, local and state government, and industry. Their concern is with improving the quality of manufacturing and service within the state. One of the best ways to improve quality is to implement total quality management (TQM). Local companies that are considering total TQM can contact the Coalition, which will put them in touch with someone who can help design, implement, and assess a TQM plan and help make contacts for local training.

COMMUNICATION.   How is this related to work in statistics? Dean explains that many contracts require a company to have a quality plan in place and that professionals with training in statistics are often called on to design, implement, and assess these plans. In fact, statisticians working in quality control may be asked to give in-house workshops to engineers and managers; Dean says it's not unlike Statistics 101 for workplace professionals.

Dean says these workshops are just one example of the importance of statisticians being able to communicate. He says it's not uncommon for employers to call him about recommending potential employees. Employers need someone who will seek business, someone who will seek opportunities to apply statistics to problems. Employers say, "If they don't have good communications skills, we can't use them."

These new emphases are becoming more important to Dean. He says, "When I step down as an administrator, I'll move more

toward TQM and statistics education as areas in which I see
myself doing scholarship in the future."

In the Workplace as an Assistant Bank Manager

Mary Beth Willis is the assistant manager at Midland Savings
Bank. The branch office where Mary Beth works is the only
Midland branch that offers all services to customers: not only full
teller services, but also financial counseling, annuities and securities, mortgages, and insurance.

BACKGROUND.   Mary Beth has had lots of on-the-job training
and continuing education because she entered a banking career
in a nontraditional way. She has a bachelor's degree in physical
education and health. Because there were no teaching positions
when she completed her undergraduate degree, she started work
at a bank that was later bought by Midland, where she currently
works. Some of the training she's completed at the Institute of
Financial Education includes seasonal updates about IRAs and
seminars about consumer loans and customer services.

RESPONSIBILITIES.   As assistant manager, Mary Beth's responsibilities include serving as consumer lending and operation supervisor; thus, she's in charge of training. She trains new personnel
as well as long-term employees about new products and services.
She supervises two staff meetings per month: one for operations
(going over any new procedures) and one for sales (coming up
with new ideas to sell existing customers as well as new business).
    Mary Beth also is responsible for bank security, which requires
training staff to handle a range of problems from customers trying
to pass bad checks to bank robbery. She makes sure that tellers
follow certain behind-the-scene procedures that protect both the
bank and the customer. For example, the bank must report
several types of transactions such as cash used to purchase over
$3,000 in traveler's checks or the withdrawal of more than
$10,000. Her position differs from an operations manager in

some other organizations because of the flexibility her position offers; with the authority and autonomy she is given, she can make her own choices about how she accomplishes her job.

As part of Mary Beth's managerial responsibilities, she is responsible for constructing a budget and for supervising the branch's task force group that considers and recommends new changes for various services. She also is responsible for writing approximately fifteen different monthly reports about topics ranging from minutes of branch office staff meetings to reports about security and consumer loans. She also writes a great many internal memos and letters to customers.

SUGGESTIONS.   Mary Beth says that someone who wants a job like hers needs to have "people skills and personality." Having a good background in human relations doesn't hurt because she has to work with a broad array of customers, handle many different kinds of problems, and motivate people. These skills are as important as her technical skills in operating various kinds of computer equipment and understanding bank policies and procedures.

CHAPTER TWELVE

Jobs with Number Crunching for Non-Number Crunchers

The careers you've read about so far are ones in which you'd expect number crunching to be part of the job. However, many people have careers that don't sound as if they'd have much to do with numbers, and people's backgrounds aren't necessarily filled with mathematics, statistics, and various numeracy-related study in computer science, engineering, or accounting. Yet some jobs have aspects that can only be done by someone who's comfortable with numbers and capable of solving simple (and sometimes not so simple) problems using a quantitative approach. Identifying all the jobs that have quantitative aspects isn't possible, but this chapter discusses people in three different careers whose successes depend in part on their ability to use mathematics even though that's not an immediately obvious part of their job.

Number Crunching in Landscape Design

Garden designers apply their artistic knowledge to the environment, using their knowledge in horticulture and art to design shapes and spaces that must blend and balance with architecture on one side and nature on the other.

In the Workplace as a Garden Designer

Margaret Burnett owns a landscape design business that specializes in creating and maintaining country estate gardens that have been featured in *House Beautiful*. Most of her customers are in northwestern Connecticut, near where she lives in Norfolk. Margaret has an associate's degree in fine arts and a bachelor's degree with honors in liberal arts and humanities, neither of which gave her much background in math. However, in her business, she uses a variety of quantitative skills: designing gardens, prepping gardens, ordering plants, billing customers, and managing quarterly and annual tax records.

As a garden designer for country estates, Margaret is initially concerned with the design layout of a garden. She considers a variety of factors in creating a design: spacing between plants and shrubs; bloom time (time, duration) and dormancy; plant height, color, and texture; and plant "friendliness" (that is, a plant's sensual qualities—Is it prickly? Is it fragrant?). But she also has to consider more quantitative factors. For example, many designers work with the broad guideline of eight plants per one hundred square feet of garden; however, Margaret adjusts this guideline according to a variety of factors such as the type and size of the plant or shrub, the exposure, and the type of soil.

When Margaret preps a garden, she cuts the shape and lays out the line of the garden, de-sods and then rototills the area, tests the soil and adds "amendments" (soil conditioners such as manure, peat, sand, organic matter, compost, lime, mulch, superphosphate or organic phosphate, chemicals, or natural fertilizers—bone meal, ash). The rates of application for soil conditioners are determined by formulas that vary with factors such as the nature of the soil, the type of conditioner, and type of application (two applications options include pounds per square foot or area or pounds per shrub or tree diameter). For example, bark mulch is spread two to three inches thick and left to lie on top of the soil; compost also is spread two to three inches thick, but it is worked into the top layer of the soil.

Many other aspects of garden design are a combination of artistic sensitivities balanced with an expert knowledge of horticulture and guided by a variety of quantitative guidelines and rules of thumb including:

- manipulative pruning (for example, to create *espalliers*);
- specialty pruning (for example, to rejuvenate, to encourage flowering or foliage, or to improve sight lines);
- selection of garden type (for example, shade or sun, wet or dry, foliage or blooms); and
- estate garden maintenance, which includes pruning, weeding, edging, fertilizing, cultivating, and grooming.

Another area of Margaret's work is common to every owner of a small business. She has to pay a variety of expenses beyond her materials for herself and her seasonal employees: worker's compensation, unemployment, social security, sales tax (6 percent labor and materials), estimated taxes, business liability insurance, and state licensing fees. In the summer, she sometimes maintains as much as $2,000 in plant stock, ready for customers' gardens. She has to calculate the price for this stock, considering her cost, which includes factors such as the wholesale or discounted price she paid, the difficulty of obtaining the plant, the special care the plant may have taken, and the garden design in which the plant will be used.

Margaret has to purchase and maintain equipment for her work—not only a truck, but smaller pieces such as a rototiller, hedge trimmer, leaf blower, leaf sucker, string trimmer, and Weed Wacker. She also has to pay membership dues for professional organizations, subscriptions for journals and trade magazines, and books for professional reference. She regularly attends professional design seminars sponsored through organizations such as the New York Botanical Garden and Arnold Arboretum.

While being a garden designer is not primarily a quantitative profession, Margaret needs to keep records—worksheets and materials lists so the bookkeeper can do the billing and so the accountant can prepare the quarterly and annual tax forms.

Number Crunching in Book Publishing

Book publishers—especially university presses—like to think that part of what they're doing is making interesting and even valuable ideas available to a broad audience.

In the Workplace as an International Marketing Director for a Publishing Company

Don Stanford is the director of international marketing at MIT Press in Cambridge, Massachusetts. Even though he has a Ph.D. in political science and has done some college teaching, he has spent the majority of his professional life working in publishing.

Most of Don's job deals with creating, maintaining, and modifying sales and promotion programs. His formal training in math is limited to algebra in high school and trigonometry and calculus in college. In graduate school, he did study statistics and computer programming (for example, FORTRAN, PLI) as part of his work on survey methodology. Although he hasn't taken a large number of math courses, he has an important characteristic typical of people who use quantitative approaches in their work: he believes that numeracy is important and that everyone should have basic math and computer skills that will help them be more effective at their job.

Many aspects of his job require simple math—for example, projection of how many MIT Press books will be sold in various countries during the coming year and construction of his annual budget. Sometimes, however, he encounters more difficult problems that require numeracy. Recently, he needed to create a data base table that would automatically provide two different prices for each of the more than two hundred new books per year that

MIT Press adds to its list: a dollar price for U.S. sales and an export price marked up by some uniform percentage over the U.S. dollar price. Unfortunately, using a standard markup often results in odd figures; for example, if the U.S. price of $9.95 was increased by a standard 12 percent markup, the new price would be $11.14. Don wanted the "cents" part of the price to be standard—25, 50, 75, 95—so he needed the computer program to automatically round the price to the nearest 25 cents, unless the price was closer to a dollar, in which case the program needed to move the price to the dollar minus 5 cents. The computer manual didn't have an easy and obvious solution and no one else in the office knew immediately how to solve the problem. Don used the existing computer functions in new ways, applying what he knew to solve this quantitative problem.

Number Crunching in School Administration

School administrators are primarily responsible for implementing the policies of the school board and assuring the smooth day-to-day operation of the school. Being a school administrator is primarily a job in organizational management, dealing with lots of people in a variety of situations.

In the Workplace as an Academic Program Coordinator

Since 1983, Kay North has been the Coordinator K–12/Resource Teacher of Gifted Students for Ames Community Schools' Extended Learning Program, which is the school district's program for talented and gifted (TAG) students. Kay really isn't a number cruncher, but two important parts of her job make number crunching a necessity.

One important responsibility is collecting, analyzing, and interpreting quantitative and qualitative analyses data to identify which children can be admitted to the program to encourage academic and creative giftedness. The data include behavioral rating sheets completed by parents and teachers of all third graders, Iowa Test of Basic Skills scores, and narrative comments from teachers to be analyzed and rank ordered. Analyses of the data give Kay some insight about students' thinking and creative abilities and enable her to present these data in a spreadsheet summary. The qualitative data deal with three categories: learning ability, motivation, and creativity. The quantitative data are based on standardized test scores. The final selection of the top 15 percent of students for the district's Extended Learning Program is made by a team of teachers for TAG students.

Another number crunching aspect of Kay's job involves creating the approximately $190,000 annual budget for the program. This budget includes line items such as salaries and benefits, instructional supplies, services, and travel. About 75 percent of this budget comes from Modified Allowable Growth, a state tax used by over 80 percent of the districts in the state to fund gifted educational programs. The remaining 25 percent of the budget is guaranteed by the local school district.

Kay's background in child development and elementary education—both a B.S. and an M.S.—and her years as a sixth grade teacher didn't emphasize the skills in quantitative analysis and budgeting that are an essential part of her current job. However, she says, "I have always been intrigued by math and science, partly as a result of my work in environmental education. And I had a mentor, a principal, who encouraged me to learn about budgeting." Kay points out that her work requires number crunching "with a human edge" so that decisions are never made solely on the basis of numbers; the people and the situations that created the numbers are always considered.

VGM CAREER BOOKS

VGM Career Horizons
a division of *NTC Publishing Group*
4255 West Touhy Avenue
Lincolnwood, Illinois 60646-1975